*Some of the Amazing
and Inspiring True Experiences
You Are About to Share:*

◇ What it feels like to die

◇ What "the Light" actually looks like

◇ Leaving the physical body during intense pain

◇ Soul travel during surgery

◇ Meeting masters, angels, teachers, and guides

◇ Projecting the human double to others

◇ Encounters with the spirits of the dead

◇ Returning to life with new powers

◇ And much more, in completely authenticated
near-death experiences of men, women, and
children from all walks of life and all over the
country, including Brad Steiger's own story.
You'll also find out what scientists and spiritual
leaders say about why such experiences occur
so often and what they mean to us today.

ONE WITH THE LIGHT

ONE

◇

WITH

◇

THE

◇

LIGHT

Brad Steiger

Ⓢ
A SIGNET BOOK

SIGNET
Published by the Penguin Group
Penguin Books USA Inc., 375 Hudson Street,
New York, New York 10014, U.S.A.
Penguin Books Ltd, 27 Wrights Lane,
London W8 5TZ, England
Penguin Books Australia Ltd, Ringwood,
Victoria, Australia
Penguin Books Canada Ltd, 10 Alcorn Avenue,
Toronto, Ontario, Canada M4V 3B2
Penguin Books (N.Z.) Ltd, 182-190 Wairau Road,
Auckland 10, New Zealand

Penguin Books Ltd, Registered Offices:
Harmondsworth, Middlesex, England

First published by Signet, an imprint of Dutton Signet,
a division of Penguin Books USA Inc.

First Printing, September, 1994
10 9 8 7 6 5 4 3 2 1

PUBLISHER'S NOTE
Although the events recounted in this book are real, the names of most
individuals have been changed to protect their privacy.

CONTENTS

• 1 •

A Glimpse of Heaven: The Near-Death Experience

I became a firm believer in the survival of the human spirit at the age of eleven when I underwent a dramatic near-death experience (NDE), and I was left with the firm conviction that the human soul is imperishable. And we need not fear death.

I have a blurred memory of losing my balance, falling off the farm tractor that I had been driving, and landing in the path of the implement with the whirling blades.

I remember pain as the machine's left tire mashed my upper body and broke my collarbone. And then I no longer felt any pain as the blades clutched at my head and ripped at my scalp and skull. I had left the body, and I was now floating many feet above the grisly scene.

I was relieved when my seven-year-old sister June, who had been riding with me, brought the tractor under control, but I was becoming more detached about such matters by the moment.

I had a sense of identification with the mangled Iowa farm boy that I saw lying bleeding beneath me on the hay stubble below, but I was growing increasingly aware that that unfortunate lad was not who I really was. The real me now seemed to be an orangish-colored ball that seemed intent only on moving steadily toward a brilliant light. At first, because of my religious orientation, I believed the illumination to be a manifestation of Jesus or an angel coming to comfort me, but I could distinguish no distinct forms or shapes within the bright emanation of light. All I seemed to feel was an urgency to become one with that magnificent light.

Strangely, though, from time to time my attention seemed to be divided between moving toward the wondrous light and descending back toward the hay field.

I opened my eyes, blinked back the blood, and became aware of my father, shocked, tears streaming down his face, carrying my body from the field.

And then I discovered a most remarkable thing: I could be in two places at once. I could exist physically in my father's arms as he carried my terribly injured body from the field; and at the same time, I could be above us, watching the whole scene as if I were a detached observer.

When I became concerned about my mother's reaction to my dreadful accident, I made an even more incredible discovery: The Real Me could be anywhere that I wished to be. My spirit, my soul, was free of the physical limitations of the human definitions of Time and Space. I had but to think of my mother, and there I was beside her as she labored in the kitchen, as yet unaware of my accident.

I put the newly found freedom to other tests. I thought of Jim, Dave, Lyle, Ralph—the friends with whom I planned to see the Roy Rogers-Gene Autrey double-feature that night in the Bode Theater. Instantly I was beside each of them as they worked with their father on their own farms.

And then I was back with Mom, trying to put my arms around her, wanting her to be able to feel me. Disappointed, I was forced to conclude that she could neither see nor feel me. My normally very attentive mother had absolutely no awareness of my spirit form.

It was August 23, Mom and Dad's anniversary. We had been trying to finish work early so that we could eat at a restaurant before the double-feature began. I had certainly given Mom and Dad a wonderful anniversary present.

And my sister! I had probably scarred her for

life. A seven-year-old girl having to watch her brother being run over and killed.

Killed. That was when it occurred to me that I was dying.

I had an awful moment of panic. I did not want to die.

I did not want to leave my mother, father, and sister.

And then the beautiful light was very near to me, and I perceived a calming intelligence, a being composed of pure light that projected before me a peculiar, three-dimensional geometric design that somehow instantly permeated my very essence with the knowledge that everything would be all right.

The very sight of that geometric design somehow transmitted to me that there was a pattern to the universe and a meaning, a Divine Plan, to life.

My panic and my fear left me, and I experienced a blissful euphoria, an incredible sense of Oneness with All That Is. I was ready to die and to become one with the light.

But even though I was at peace with what appeared to be the fast-approaching reality of death, I had misinterpreted the reason why the intelligence within the light had shown me the geometric representation of the Divine Plan. It seems that an integral part of my mission on Earth was to testify to others about what I had been shown.

About 1982, I was attempting to describe the geometric design to a number of other men and women who had undergone near-death experiences. When I found myself unable to provide a meaningful description of the pattern, I stated that the design—so clearly envisioned by me to this day—appeared to be ineffable, beyond human description. Three or four of the group stated that they understood what I was attempting to explain, for they, too, had been shown some kind of tranquilizing, yet revelatory, geometric object—and they also found it impossible to describe it in mere words.

It was not until 1988 when my wife, Sherry Hansen Steiger, began to conduct healing seminars utilizing computer-derived images of fractal geometry that I saw designs that very closely approximated what I had been shown during my near-death experience.

In the August 12, 1973 issue of the *National Enquirer,* our former family physician, Dr. Cloyce A. Newman, was interviewed about my near-death experience that had occurred twenty-six years before. Dr. Newman, who was at that time living in retirement in Homestead, Florida, told of his shock when my father carried me into his office and how he had had me rushed by car to St. Mary's Hospital in Des Moines, about 140 miles away: "He was very seriously injured and on the verge of death. We managed to get him to a specialist and it saved his life."

I was in and out of the body during those 140 miles, and I did not come back with any serious intention of staying in that domicile of flesh until the surgery was about to begin. At that point, it seemed as though some energy was insisting that I return to participate in the medical procedure. I came back with such force that I sat up, shouted, and knocked an intern off-balance. I continued to struggle until the soft voice of a Roman Catholic sister pacified me long enough for the anesthesia to take effect. Although my life force remained in the eleven-year-old body to cooperate with the surgery, my Real Self left to spend the next twelve hours in a delightful park in another dimension, complete with bandstand, ice cream vendors, and smiling, pleasant people.

From the perspective of my now fifty-eight years, I can see that my near-death experience at the age of eleven was a most fortunate one. Certainly one of the questions that every thinking man and woman eventually asks is, "Is there life after physical death?" I was blessed to have that eternal puzzler answered for me in the affirmative before I entered my teens.

I was shown through my powerful near-death experience that there is an essential part of us, perhaps most commonly referred to as the soul, that does survive physical death. This knowledge has greatly influenced my attitude toward life, as well as toward death.

And I am far from alone in having been granted this emancipating awareness, this life-altering assurance.

Since 1968, I have distributed questionnaires to readers of my books and to my lecture and workshop audiences. Of the more than 20,000 people who have returned completed forms—55 percent state that they have had a near-death experience; 74 percent report out-of-body experiences; 72 percent claim an illumination experience.

"I know what a beautiful life is waiting for us when we end our present life. I don't fear death. I'm not in a hurry to return to Heaven, but I know it is something to look forward to."

These are not words of faith in a promised after-life for the human soul, but a testimony of reassurance that such a state truly exists—and Patricia Gleason feels that she has the experience to back up her statement.

In January, 1944, Queen Elizabeth Hospital in Birmingham, England, opened its operating room doors to Mrs. Gleason so that she might have a cancerous growth removed from her stomach. The operation was considered very risky because it involved cutting away much of her stomach, but she knew that it was necessary.

Sometime during the six-hour surgery, Patricia Gleason became convinced that she died.

"I felt myself suddenly floating above the operating table, looking down at the team of able men and women working over my body," she said. Her pain was gone, and she felt marvelously at peace.

At this point, she later recalled, she was "walking through space," without registering any feelings.

The next thing she knew, she was walking along a road, but she could not feel her feet touching the ground. Double wrought-iron gates impeded her progress. She could see someone looking at her through the gates—so she simply passed through them.

On the other side there was an unseen source of illumination that brought out the colors of flowers, grass, and trees more intensely than Patricia had ever before experienced.

And then she was standing before her mother, Mrs. Anne Bishop, who had passed away in 1941 at the age of sixty-four. Just before her mother had died, she had been forced to have her left leg amputated due to gangrene, but when Patricia saw her now, she had both of her legs and appeared to be many years younger.

"I walked up to her, and she held up her hand," Patricia remembers. "I stopped. She shook her head from side to side and said, 'Not yet, not yet.'

"Then I couldn't see my mother anymore. I

felt myself floating back through darkness. The next day I woke up in my hospital bed."

Later that day, Patricia spoke with a nurse who had been in the operating room with her during the surgery and who confirmed her strong conviction that she had actually died during the surgical procedure. According to the nurse, Patricia's heart had stopped, and in the minutes before its beat could be stimulated back into life-sustaining action, she had been technically dead.

"I have never feared the thought of dying since then," Patricia Gleason said. "Before my strange but wonderful experience with the world beyond, I had only feelings of fear and dread concerning death. But all that has changed for me. The fear is gone, and in its place is a feeling that life after death is pleasant—and that it is something that I can look forward to with calm anticipation."

Patricia Gleason firmly believes that she made a short visit to the world beyond death, and she unhesitatingly affirms that her brief sojourn there will affect the remainder of her life on this planet.

She Didn't Want to Return to Her Physical Body

Heidi Anderson was left in terrible pain after her surgery on July 20, 1968. Although her surgery had been relatively minor, as she lay in her hospital bed she became convinced that something must have gone wrong and that she must be dying.

In a letter to me, Heidi wrote: "Just at the point where I was about to reach for the bulb by my pillow and flash for the nurse, I had an odd sensation, like my feet, my legs, my body were being rolled up like a giant toothpaste tube.

"Then my *real* self seemed to be all rolled up in a corner of my skull. There was a really intense spasm of pain—and then I seemed to shoot up into a corner of the room."

Heidi was convinced that she had died. "For a fleeting moment I felt upset and angered at the injustice of dying as the result of such a minor operation. I morosely attributed my death to the inadequacies of the hospital staff and the incompetence of my doctor.

"Then a warm wave of peace seemed to wash over me, and I thought how foolish it was to care about a continued existence in that painfully throbbing shell of flesh that lay sprawled out on the hospital bed below me."

She was appalled at her appearance. "My cheeks seemed drawn, and my eye sockets looked hollow. My eyes were closed, and I studied myself for a bit, because I had never been able to imagine what I would look like with my eyes closed. I looked horrible."

Heidi saw a nurse come into the hospital

room. "She must have just come on duty, because I had not seen her around before. I at once had an impression of a very conscientious and responsible woman, who, though efficient, went about her work with compassion.

"She took one look at my body lying on the bed, and I perceived a flash of anxiety and concern.

"She called for orderlies, interns, and other nurses; and they all started working over my body.

"At first I thought: 'Oh, no, you don't! I don't want to return to my body! I like it just fine up here in a corner of the room!'"

But then Heidi began to feel guilty as wave after wave of anxiety and concern began to buffet her from the group of medical personnel who were desperately striving to bring her back to physical life.

"Then one of them gave me a powerful injection of *something,* and I began to feel myself being drawn back toward my physical body.

"It seemed as though there was an opening on the top of my skull. I rolled myself back up—and I aimed myself like a bullet for that hole."

Heidi remembered that everyone smiled when she opened her eyes.

"But I knew that I had only come back to awful pain," she concluded her account of the experience.

Food-Poisoning Sent Him Out-of-the-Body to Escape the Agony

Arnold Sandeen of Utah added this account of his near-death encounter when he returned his Steiger Questionnaire of Mystical, Paranormal, and UFO Experience:

"When I was about seventeen, I awakened one evening with what I thought was a terrible case of indigestion as a result of having eaten too much at a school picnic.

"Although I tried not to disturb my sleeping parents, the absolutely unbearable pain caused me to moan and cry out, and soon my mother was at my bedside. She diagnosed the symptoms as being indicative of appendicitis and she called Dr. Radnich."

As he lay thrashing about in agony, Arnold's thoughts began to fixate on the possibility of being somehow able to escape the pain that seemed to fill every corner of his being. How wonderful it would be to be able to leave his torment, he said mentally.

"Just then a spasm of pain doubled me over, and the reflex action seemed to shoot the *thinking part of me* up to the ceiling. I thought, 'Oh, no! I wanted to be able to escape the pain, but I didn't want to die!' "

Arnold was completely astonished. He could actually see his mother fussing about, and he could clearly perceive himself tossing about on the bed, moaning and groaning.

"My body seemed to be like some kind of puppet, just going through the motions of awful sickness. But I—the *Real Me*—could no longer feel a thing. Incredibly, the pain remained down below with my physical body on the bed.

"Then I started feeling kind of ashamed about the way my physical body was behaving like such a baby. I mean, the pain was awful and all; but I was whimpering and moaning like a wimp. I decided that I really should go back and act like a man."

And just like that, Arnold said that he was back in his physical body and howling in pain.

"If it hurt so bad to be in my body—and there was absolutely no pain when I was outside of my body—then it didn't take a genius like me very long to decide where I wanted to be."

Arnold was surprised to discover how quickly the *Real Arnold* was able to be back up floating near the ceiling.

He wondered when Doc Radnich was going to get there—and suddenly he was inside the doctor's car as he traveled to the Sandeen home.

After he had ridden with the doctor for a few minutes, Arnold thought once again of his mother's anxiety, and he was back in his room.

"Mom was crying, and when I looked at my body, I could see why. I looked hideous. My face was gray and my mouth was hanging open—and I didn't seem to be breathing!"

Arnold experienced just a moment of panic

when it occurred to him that he might truly have died.

"But then I looked behind me and saw this really beautiful being of pure light that seemed to be waiting for me on the other side of a crystal clear river. Somehow I understood that all I had to do was to cross over the bridge and join the Light Being—and that would be all there was to it.

"I guess like so many teenagers I had never really thought much about dying. And I certainly had never thought that it could happen to me. At least not until I was an old guy, like fifty or so. But if this was all there was to it, then it was hard to understand why people always made such a big deal about dying. You just 'pop' out of your body, maybe float around the ceiling for a while, then meet some beautiful angel who's waiting for you on the other side of the bridge between life and death. It's really no big deal at all!"

And then, all of a sudden, Arnold seemed to be being drawn away from the crystal river, the bridge, and the Light Being and pulled toward his physical body.

"I seemed to land hard on something, and I opened my eyes to see Dad standing with his arm around Mom's shoulder. Doc Radnich's face seemed to be really close to my eyes, and I could hear Dad cussing him out for having taken so long to get there.

"Everything went out of focus, then black for a while; and when I opened my eyes again, I could hear Mom crying and praying and thanking God that I had come back to life.

"I was sick for three or four more days. Doc said it was probably some spoiled meat that I ate at the school picnic. I know now that death is not such a terrible thing," Arnold concluded his account, "but I really am not in any hurry to cross that bridge, either."

The Golden Light Met Him at the Entrance to the "Gateway" Between Worlds

In the November 1993 issue of *Guideposts* magazine, Martin Bauer of Worcester, Massachusetts, described his near-death experience when he was a nineteen-year-old sneaking a visit to his younger brother, who was quarantined in camp because of a strep-throat epidemic.

Martin had climbed a tree sixty-five feet up to shout a hello to Andy. They arranged a time and place to meet along the waterfront the next morning.

Then, a few moments later, the branches that he had been grasping so firmly "suddenly snapped off with a *crack*."

The nineteen-year-old hurtled through the air, desperately flailing arms and legs, hoping for something to break his fall.

Then the lights went out.

Martin Bauer wrote that he now floated in "a world of gray." If he was dreaming, it was the most vivid dream that he had ever experienced:

"I do not know where I am. This world is gray, but it has a depth and is distinct, like the overcast grayness of clouds rolling over the mountains of northern New England."

After an indeterminate passing of time, Martin sensed something to his left: "A golden light appears. Gradually it pushes the gray away. My curiosity intensifies as the light grows brighter, but try as I might I cannot shift faster to see its source. Slowly, ever so slowly, I understand that what is out of sight is not a something but a someone—a presence, radiating a tremendous force of warmth and love, divine joy. Joy swells in my heart, and I know this is no dream. My excitement soars as I struggle to reach the light, so full of life and peace."

Martin Bauer regained consciousness lying on a bed of grass and soft pine needles. For what he estimated to be the next five hours he was in and out of consciousness.

Taking stock of his situation, he knew that Andy had not seen him fall and since the camp was quarantined, no one was likely to be out in the woods. He realized that, injured though he was, he was on his own.

When he momentarily felt panic sweep over him, he remembered his experience with the light. Would he have been drawn back from the "gateway" if he had not been meant to live?

Somehow controlling the terrible pain, Martin hobbled the several hundred yards down to the lake, where his calls for help were eventually heard.

Later, he learned that he had broken both of his arms, fractured his right hip, shattered the bone around his right eye, severely bruised four ribs on the right side of his chest, and nearly punctured a lung.

Throughout his terrible ordeal, Martin Bauer stated that his brief encounter at the "gateway" sustained him ". . . even as it sustains me today. For this I give thanks to God."

He Climbed a Marble Staircase to the Other Side

It was in 1957 that Bertram Frace was knocked off a crane at a steel plant near Trenton, New Jersey. He suffered severe head injuries and was rushed to Lower Bucks County Hospital in Levittown, Pennsylvania, where he lay in a coma for nine days.

"I recall it all vividly," Frace said, "even though it happened to me back in 1957.

First, Frace said, he had a strange feeling of separation from his physical body, then he found himself ascending a marble stairway that seemed to stretch into the clouds.

"I started to climb that marble staircase out of

curiosity. It seemed as though I climbed those marble stairs for days. The stairs kept going up through the clouds until the atmosphere became buoyant and vibrant.

"I sat down to rest on one occasion, then started to climb again. Suddenly I heard a voice, faint at first, then a little stronger, saying, 'Bertram, go back.'

"I looked around me in bewilderment, but I could see no one."

Puzzled, Bertram called out to the source of the mysterious voice, "Who are you? Where are you?"

Again the voice spoke, louder this time, harsher: "Bertram, you listen to me and go back down those stairs!"

"All at once I realized that I was hearing the voice of my grandmother, who had died four years earlier," Bertram said.

Still unable to see his grandmother, Bertram protested to the bodiless voice: "But, Grandma, I need to see where these stairs go."

Grandmother's voice became even more insistent, and she began to sound very cross: "No, Bertram, they're not ready for you yet. Go back. You have two children who need you."

It was at that moment that Frace began to come out of his coma.

His eyes fluttered open, and he saw his wife and his two sons standing at his bedside.

A few days later, when he was feeling better,

his doctor told him that he had nearly been given up for dead. On several occasions, while he was unconscious and in the coma, he had skirted dangerously close to death.

The Research of Dr. Kubler-Ross and Dr. Moody Affirms Life After Death

In the late 1970s, the popular acceptance of the work of Dr. Elisabeth Kubler-Ross brought sharp scientific focus to bear on the question of what happens to us after the experience of physical death. In her book, *Death, the Final Stages of Growth,* Dr. Kubler-Ross declares that "beyond a shadow of a doubt, there is life after death."

Far from an evangelical tract, Dr. Kubler-Ross's volume is actually a textbook which is based on more than a thousand interviews with terminally ill persons, many of whom had recovered from near-death experiences. They describe such sensations as floating above their own bodies and being able to transcend the normally accepted physical limitations of Time and Space. Nearly all told of a sense of euphoria and peace, and many had been confronted by angels and spirit beings who told them that it was not yet time for them to make the final transition to the other side.

When the dying do accomplish that ultimate change of dimensions, according to Dr. Kubler-

Ross's observations, they are ". . . at peace; they are fully awake; when they float out of their bodies they are without fear, pain, or anxiety; and they have a sense of wholeness."

Dr. Raymond Moody discovered an enormous number of similar reports when he became curious about what happened to patients in the period of time in which they "died" before being revived and returned to life through medical treatment. After interviewing many men and women who had had such experiences (*Life After Life*) Dr. Moody found what Dr. Kubler-Ross and numerous other researchers (such as Dr. Karlis Osis of the American Society for Psychical Research) had discovered:

*They have the sensation of moving rapidly through a long, dark tunnel before "popping" outside of their physical bodies. If they are in hospital rooms or other enclosures, they often float near the ceiling and watch the medical teams attempting to revive their physical bodies.

*Many reported their life literally "flashing" before their eyes.

*They are often welcomed to the other world by previously deceased friends or relatives.

*Whether or not they are of a "churched" or religious background, they often report an encounter with a brilliant, intense white light that has the form of an angel, a guide, a teacher, Father Abraham, or a Christ-figure.

Dr. Moody, who is both a medical doctor

and the holder of a doctorate in philosophy, emphasizes that he is not attempting to "sell" a point of view; but he freely confesses that after talking with hundreds of men and women who have had the near-death experience, he personally does not doubt that there is survival of bodily death.

• 2 •

The Hand of an Angel Turned Her Back to Life

Mrs. Dorothy Forbeck of Akron, Ohio, was admitted into the hospital on June 12, 1978, for the birth of her third child, Esther. The delivery became extremely difficult, and the resulting pain caused Dorothy to undergo a near-death experience.

"Because of this experience," she said, "I know that death should hold no horror for any of us."

Dorothy Forbeck's pregnancy had from the onset been complicated by her abnormally high blood pressure. Then, during the course of the birth-giving process, she lost a great deal of blood.

Two days after the birth of Esther, while lying

on her hospital bed, a strange sensation crept over her.

"I felt excruciating pain," she recalled. "Then I felt faint and breathless. I was certain that I was dying when I could feel myself leaving my body and floating up to the ceiling."

Dorothy clearly recalled looking down and gazing at her pale, motionless body upon the hospital bed. She fleetingly paused to worry about the shock some member of the hospital staff would undergo when he or she would find her dead. She experienced another moment of anguish when she foresaw the sorrow of her husband, who would now be left with two young sons and a newborn daughter.

"Then I drifted away into darkness—until I found myself in a different world," she said.

Dorothy next felt a tingling sensation, and she could distinctly feel ". . . the hands of small children holding my arms, guiding me. I was floating, not walking. It was dark for quite some time, and then I saw a light in front of me. I somehow knew that I was to continue floating toward the light."

Once she had passed through the light, she found herself walking along a pleasant green slope that was bathed in a soft illumination from the beautiful light. It was a lovely scene, and Dorothy felt no desire to leave it.

"There was no fear or pain. There were all kinds of flowers around me. It was just too beautiful to leave, but I saw before me some huge gates and I began to walk toward them. I instinctively knew that Heaven, Paradise, Jesus, Mother Mary, and all the saints lived in the magnificent city that lay behind the massive gates. I knew the city must be Heaven, because I could see tall golden spires, parapets, and towers stretching up behind the gates. At this point, I felt as though I were walking, but I couldn't feel my feet touch the ground."

All at once, Dorothy Forbeck felt a "huge hand" on her shoulder, holding her back and restraining her movement toward the gates.

"I looked over my shoulder and beheld a tall, powerful-looking angel, whose face was both loving and stern," she said. "His countenance glowed with heavenly light, and when he spoke my entire spirit being vibrated with his words: 'You must not go any farther. You must not enter the gates of the heavenly kingdom. It is not yet your time!' "

Dorothy admitted that she struggled against the hand of the angel guardian. "I felt so disappointed that I had been halted before I had entered Heaven. But I could do nothing to stop the hand of the angel from leading me away from the gates to Paradise."

Protest as she might, the angel led her back to her body, back through the darkness and back to the pain.

"On the Other Side, the pain that I had felt

after the delivery was gone, and I didn't want to return to it," Dorothy said. "But as the angel led me away from the heavenly gates, and I felt myself drifting back into my physical body, all the pain began to come back."

As consciousness returned more completely, Dorothy experienced feelings of great exhaustion, as though she had just been on a long journey. But she knew that she was back in her physical body and that everything was now going to be all right.

A nurse making her rounds stopped to talk with her, and Dorothy told her of her remarkable journey.

"The nurse said that I had been very ill and that for a while they feared that they might lose me," Dorothy said. "She also went on to say that she had spoken to other patients who had undergone experiences very much like mine."

Dorothy remarked that as Esther grew older she had become troubled by the fact that her delivery had nearly cost her mother her life.

"I told her that she should never have such thoughts," Dorothy explained. "I told her that the experience was really very pleasant and enormously reassuring, and there was no reason for her to worry about it.

"Most importantly, I reminded her that now that I have seen what it is like on the other side, I will not fear going there again when my time *does* come to walk through the massive gates of the heavenly city."

• 3 •

It Was Not Yet Her Time

In February of 1983, Shirley Tangelli of Denver, Colorado, lay critically ill in her home. Her doctor had given her medication, but her recent pneumonia attack had been so severe that no member of her family expected her to live through the night.

Unknown to Shirley, her temperature was dangerously high. What she did understand without question was that she felt miserably ill and that she had great difficulty in breathing.

Although she did not know the exact hour and minute, sometime "in the middle of the night" she felt that some very essential part of her total being was beginning to slip out of her physical body.

"It was very strange," she said later, "but I was not afraid. It just happened that my soul left my body, and I was not even worried about it."

The next thing of which she was aware was that she was moving through a "dark railway tunnel." Far off in the distance she could see a tiny point of light.

"I came out into the light, and I saw a green railway embankment on each side of a green road," Shirley said. "The banks were covered with lilies and the fragrance was beautiful."

Since Shirley Tangelli was experiencing her out-of-body journey during the dead of winter, she especially noticed and appreciated the heavy growth of fragrant flowers.

At the end of the road, she was delighted to see her maternal grandmother, Angie Waldrum, who had been dead for seven years.

"As soon as I saw Gram, all the pain and suffering from my long illness vanished," Shirley remembered. "After weeks of suffering, I was completely and totally free of agony and discomfort.

"I walked quickly up to Gram. It was odd. I knew that I was walking but I could feel nothing under my feet!"

As Shirley approached her grandmother, Gram Waldrum held out her arms to her.

"I longed to be enfolded in those arms once more," Shirley said, "but the nearer she came, the more insistent a sudden and unidentifiable voice became, telling me: '*Don't go yet. You are not ready!*' "

Shirley Tangelli paused, disconcerted. She looked to her grandmother to see what effect the command of the mysterious voice was having on her.

"Gram was still smiling and holding out her arms to me, but the voice spoke again, even louder than before: '*Do not go to her. It is not yet your time!*' I knew that I must return."

As soon as Shirley accepted the edict that she must go back to her physical body, she had a keen sense of some of the pain beginning to return.

"I turned and walked back into the darkness. As I passed the lilies, their edges curled and turned brown as if they were dying."

It was at this point, Shirley explained, that all the pain rushed back upon her agony-wearied body. She found that her feet were hurting as she walked the path, whereas previously she had felt not even the slightest discomfort. She kept plodding on, however, back through the tunnel, back to her physical body.

"I came to in my body, fully conscious, the crisis passed, and somehow knowing that I would return to complete health," Shirley said.

"I also knew clearly that I had passed into the next world, but I was drawn back because it was not yet my time. Had I ignored the commanding voice and gone on instead of turning back, I think it is likely that I would have never returned."

• 4 •

During the Pain of Childbirth, She Felt the Comforting Hand of Jesus

In a lengthy letter to me dated June 20, 1976, Carli Van Buren told of the painful delivery that she underwent which brought her the remarkable bonus of seeing what she believed to be the reassuring image of Jesus.

Carli wrote that she knew that she would have a difficult delivery. The doctors had debated whether or not they should take the child through Caeserean section, but they decided to wrestle with the breeched baby in the delivery room. Carli was advised that she would be given only a mild painkiller. They could not give her a general anesthetic, because she would have to help.

"Then the worst happened," she said. "My

doctor was out of town when the labor pains began. He had planned to be back in time, but my baby wouldn't wait.

"To complicate matters and make them even worse, the pediatrician with whom my doctor had discussed my case in the unforeseen event that something should prevent his being there was in the midst of a very serious surgical procedure and absolutely could not be disturbed.

"I am sorry to report that the doctor summoned at the last minute to assist me was not the best example that one might find of the devoted practitioner. He seemed hardly interested in the potential difficulty of my delivery—or in alleviating any of my pain.

"When the dilation had neared completion, the birth agony was driving me out of my mind," Carli continued her account of her ordeal. "And maybe that was just what happened, for I suddenly felt a weird whirling sensation, like I was a propeller on an airplane!"

Carli seemed to spin faster and faster ". . . and then—pop! I was floating over the bed in the labor room, looking down on my body and the nurse who sought to ease my pain."

She was shocked to see how contorted her facial features appeared. "At first I thought I must have died, but then the body on the bed below began to thresh about wildly and let out a terrible cry of pain."

Carli was really baffled. That was definitely

she down on the bed, writhing in what was obviously awful agony. But it was also she up near the ceiling, watching the scene below, feeling absolutely no pain at all.

"I saw the nurse measure my dilation. 'You're ready honey!' she said. 'Now where is that damn doctor?' "

The nurse left the room, and Carli followed her down the corridor.

"I watched her find the straying, disinterested doctor; and I saw him scowl at the interruption, as if his conversation about baseball with one of the interns was too important to be disrupted by such a minor occurrence as the birth of my baby."

Then, almost simultaneous with her observation of the doctor's distasteful scowl, Carli found herself back in the delivery room, moaning with the terrible pain. She wished that she could go back up near the ceiling again where there was no pain.

She did leave her body again during the delivery. "I saw my face so pale and glistening with sweat. Then the baby came—a beautiful boy, our Carl—and I saw that everything was all right."

For the first time in hours, she thought of her husband Jarvin, who had been sitting anxiously in the waiting room.

"Just like that," Carli wrote, "I was hovering over him, watching him play a nervous game of solitaire."

That was when Carli feared that she was about to make the final and ultimate trip from her physical body.

"While I was watching Jarv and wanting to tell him about our beautiful baby boy, I became aware of a tugging, a pulling, and I seemed to be being dragged into some kind of dark, dark tunnel."

Although she could see a light at the far end of the tunnel, Carli was frightened.

"I thought, 'Oh, no! I get through the terrible agony of the delivery—and now I die!' "

She fought an awful moment of panic, and then she perceived a glowing light beginning to form in the darkness of the tunnel.

"The light began to coalesce into a humanoid-type figure. I could begin to distinguish a face—eyes, mouth, nose. I thought for certain that it was my guardian angel coming to take me into the light.

"But then the image became that of Jesus—or at least my concept of how Jesus looks. I may not have the standard belief of certain regular churchgoers, but I have never doubted that Jesus exists somewhere in some dimension of time and space. And now, strange as it may seem to some people, Jesus stood there before me.

"His eyes were warm and kind, and I felt an overwhelming peace permeate every aspect of my being. His voice was soft and gentle.

"It is not yet your time to come home, Carli,'

he told me. 'Return to your body and to your baby. Remember that Divine Love is the one great power that moves the universe. Without it, there could not exist the wonderful harmony that exists in the celestial world of the spirit. Feel my Divine Love flowing from me to your heart, mind, and soul. From this day forward, manifest the harmony of Divine Love in your thought, word, and deed and do all that you can to bring about happiness in the hearts of all those with whom you share your life.' "

Carli saw the image of Jesus raise his hand in the universal sign of peace and farewell. Just before his form disappeared, she heard him say: "Return now, my child. Return to your Earth body feeling better, more positive, more loving than you have felt in months."

The next thing Carli knew, she had opened her eyes, and a nurse was bending over her.

"Hey," the nurse smiled. "Where are you? Did you leave us for a while? We were beginning to get worried about you."

"I guess I really was gone for a while," Carli concluded in her letter. "I was gone in a way that the nurse might not be able to imagine. But for me, I returned with a renewed spirit and a heart that was filled with rejoicing. The terrible pain of the delivery had been well worth its results: a beautiful new soul and the blessing of the Master Jesus."

• 5 •

A Buffer Against the Tragedies of Life

Mrs. Helen DeDolce of Allentown, Pennsylvania, is convinced that while she lay dying after an appendicitis operation she entered into a world beyond our own.

Her appendix had ruptured, and she had been rushed to the hospital for emergency blood transfusions. Dimly, she was aware of several doctors struggling to save her life.

"I can distinctly remember seeing myself floating above my body as I lay on a hospital bed in Allentown Hospital," she recalled in the July 1, 1969 issue of the *National Enquirer*. "I felt light as a feather—as if I were detached from my sickbed below. It was a pleasant sensation."

According to Mrs. DeDolce's account of her

near-death experience, she was traveling toward a bright light—and the celestial music that she heard was more beautiful than any that she had ever heard on Earth, before or since.

"I soon recovered, but I never forgot that experience. Since then I've lost a husband and a small child. If I had never had that near-death experience, I would have gone to pieces when they died. My experience helped me to bear up under these tragedies."

Helen DeDolce was pregnant with her fifth child when her husband Stephen died of a heart attack at the wheel of his car. The family provider was only forty-one years old.

After his death, Helen said that she cried herself to sleep for several nights.

"One night I was wishing desperately that I could see Stephen again just once more. Suddenly there he was in the room. He looked relaxed and happy. He leaned over and kissed me, then faded away."

Helen underwent yet another mystical experience when she was forced to shoulder the tragedy of her six-year-old daughter's death from leukemia. Little Michelle had been ill for quite some time, and Helen had moved the child's bed into her own room so that she might more immediately attend to her daughter's needs.

"One evening as I lay on the bed, I saw a nun in a white habit standing in a corner of my room," she said. "The nun had an angelic expression, and her hands were extended as if in compassion. I knew then that my little Michelle would die soon."

The next day, the girl had to be taken to the hospital. She received the finest medical care available, but within two months she was dead.

"I've always kept these things to myself until recently," Helen DeDolce confessed. "I used to think that people would laugh at me if I talked about them. But after thinking it over, I thought that it might help others in grief to hear my story."

Helen affirmed that she truly believes that she will meet her husband Stephen and her daughter Michelle in the afterlife which she herself once entered.

"It's been a difficult struggle bringing up the children without their father," she said, "but I am sure that I've had help from the beyond."

• 6 •

Angels Define the Light and Their Purpose During a Woman's Near-Death Experience

Gloria Novara, a correspondent of mine from San Antonio, reported her near-death experience while under the surgeon's scalpel.

"I knew all along that my doctor had lied to me," she began her account. "Perhaps his intentions were honorable. Perhaps he had only meant to keep my morale high. But now that he had cut me open, I could see by the look in his eyes that he was shocked that the cancer had spread even farther than he had supposed.

"Of course, he might not ever believe that I was looking directly into his eyes at that very moment, for I was under deep anesthetic. But I was also dying, and I was out of my body, floating up toward the ceiling."

Gloria stated that she now perceived herself as if she were a shiny orange balloon with a silver string attached to it.

"I could clearly see my body below me, but I didn't really want to watch them cutting and slicing away at me, so I did not resist when I felt something pulling me higher, farther away from the operating room.

"I thought of my husband and my three-year-old daughter in the waiting room, and I felt sad that I was leaving them—for I was convinced that I was dying. But I also knew that I would no longer have to feel any more sickness or pain.

"I heard bells tolling, like they do after funerals; and then I saw my guardian angel coming down through the ceiling for me."

The angelic being accompanied Gloria toward a bright light that appeared to be shining in the center of a great expanse of darkness.

"It was the most beautiful and compelling light that I had ever seen. My angel nodded at me as I hesitated to draw nearer. 'Yes,' the angelic being said. 'We must now become One with the Light so that we may ascend higher.'

"I felt myself blending with the powerful energy of the Light, and it was as if my very essence were being separated layer by layer. It was as though I were this orange-colored balloon-onion kind of thing, and I was being peeled layer by layer. And it was wonderful! Like each layer of my essence was being bathed in soft, warm soapy love."

The next thing Gloria Novara knew, she was no longer a shiny orange "balloon kind of thing," but she was herself again.

"I had on a lovely white robe, and all around me were beautiful angels in bright, shining gowns. They just seemed to be glowing with an inner radiance.

"And then I was blessed beyond thoughts of comprehension when Mary, the mother of Jesus, suddenly appeared in the midst of the angels. I fell to my knees, and I began to weep.

" 'You can stay her for a while, my daughter,' she said in a soft, gentle voice, 'but then you must go back.' "

Mary motioned to Gloria to follow her, and she and the group of angels walked with her into a beautiful area of flowers, green grass, and a small stream. When Mary rested near a large tree, Gloria and the angelic beings formed a small circle around her.

"Although you have become One with the Light here on one of the heavenly spheres," Mary said to Gloria, "you have always walked in the spiritual light, even while you were on Earth."

Gloria acknowledged that she had always tried to be a good Catholic.

Mary smiled. "Yes, my child, that is fine. But the spiritual light does not belong exclusively to any one religious expression. I must walk on now, but these lovely angels will explain certain spiritual matters more completely for your benefit."

Gloria said that Mary disappeared in the twinkling of an eye, and she was left seated on the green grass near the tranquil stream.

"When we angels come down to your material sphere, we can easily see which of you humans have the spiritual light within you," one of the heavenly beings told her.

Another angel spoke up and said that it was such beacons of light that aided them in finding their way about on Earth. "And such lights certainly help us to find those to whom we are assigned to minister."

Gloria was told what a privilege it was that she had been permitted to advance to the Greater Light and to become One with its beauty.

"The beauty of this Light is the beauty of Holiness," one of the benevolent beings said. "It is past the imagining of mortals, but it can also be attained by a regular practice of meditation. And be certain to keep a memory of the Light in your mind when things become difficult on Earth."

Speaking of things being difficult on Earth, Gloria asked the angels why—since Earth was going through such terrible times—they didn't appear as often to humans as they did in biblical times.

One of the heavenly beings was quick to answer. "Angels rarely come to the earth plane with the intention of 'appearing' to humans. We work always for humans and are present always in some dimension of being. But we seldom visibly appear in our actual forms.

"We may assume other physical identities. We may even temporarily occupy the physical being of another human, but we may not appear as angelic beings unless it be for some very rare and special assignment."

Gloria said that she had always wondered about the Old Testament story of Jacob wrestling with an angel. Could a man really wrestle with an angelic entity?

"Yes," another angel told her, "the account of Jacob and the angel is true, and the wrestling was real on the physical level. But understand, of course, that an angel may not be touched with impunity. This particular angel had manifested in physical and visible form out of consideration for his human ward. You will remember that the angel's slightest touch dislocated Jacob's thigh. This angel had such great love for his ward that he extended a very rare courtesy to a mortal.

"Jacob, you see, required a kind of physical act to accompany the spiritual blessing that he sought so desperately. So the angel wrestled with him as a kind of stimulus to accompany the blessing that he would have gladly and willingly bestowed anyway."

Gloria pointed out that the angel blessed Jacob, but would not give him his name.

"Angels seldom give humans their names," she was told. "There is much power in an angel's name. Know this and understand this, for great disasters may ensue from misusing holy names."

Another angel added to the reply: "Another reason that we rarely provide our names is due to the human failing of attempting to worship us or to call us to do their biding. We are never to be worshipped, for to God alone is the glory. And we are not to be summoned for such low level activities as magic or sorcery."

Gloria was confused. Was she never to be able to call upon her angels for strength or guidance?

"You must never make unwise demands of us," she was told. "The lessons of life are best learned if you learn to make use of your own resources, thus rising to greater strength by so doing. As the Scriptures say, 'The Lord knows what ye have need of.' We are always with you, providing you with inspiration and guidance from the unseen dimensions. But we are not to accomplish your lessons for you."

Gloria said that she understood. "How beautiful Heaven is. How wonderful it is to be able to have this blessing."

"This is not the true Heaven," one of the angels cautioned her. "This is a construct that we have created for your good and your gaining. It is our intention that this experience will contribute greatly to the positive growth of your soul."

"But enough of our instructions," another of the beings smiled. "We know that while you are here on the outer edge of Heaven, you would like to see someone."

"My parents!" Gloria said at once.

"Of course," the angels said in unison.

Gloria said that in another "twinkling of an eye" her beloved parents, Manuel and Felicia, manifested before her.

"We all wept tears of joy at our heavenly reunion. Neither of them looked as old as they had at their time of physical death. Both of them appeared as I remembered them from my childhood."

Gloria wrote in her account of her near-death experience that it seemed as though she spent two or three days visiting with her parents in the heavenly realm.

"Then my angelic guide, the same entity who had ascended with me to the Light, knocked at the door of the lovely little house where my parents and I had been staying and told me that it was time to return.

"No sooner had my guardian angel told me this when I was bobbing near the ceiling of a hospital room.

"I was shocked to hear Father Sanchez below me, giving my body the last rites. My husband lay across my feet crying, and I somehow knew that my sister was outside in the hall with my daughter. A nurse stood at the left side of the bed, her fingers on my pulse."

At this point, Gloria said that she received another image of Mother Mary. "You could only stay for a little while," she said. "It was not yet your time to remain. But remember well all the lessons that you have received in the heavenly realm."

There was a strange, crackling noise, and Gloria saw the color of blood all around her.

"I realized after a few moments that I was back in my physical body. I moaned with the pain of my illness and the surgery.

"When I opened my eyes, my husband and Father Sanchez were smiling, and the nurse had just reentered the room with our doctor."

Gloria weakly found her voice and told them that she had been to Heaven and had spoken with Mother Mary and a group of angels.

Father Sanchez said that he did not doubt that she had gone somewhere far away, for the doctors at the hospital had only given her a few minutes more to either pass the crisis or pass on to another world. He had been called upon to administer the last rites, because her chances to live had seemed very slim.

"Our doctor told me that they were certain that they had been able to remove all the cancer and that it should be a good long time before I returned to Heaven," Gloria said.

"My husband, sister, and daughter all loudly proclaimed their joy that I had been returned from the arms of the angels to their own loving arms."

Later, Gloria wrote in her account of the experience, she told her sister in detail of her visit with their parents in the heavenly realm.

"My sister agrees with me that my experience was genuine, and she has asked me to share all of the angelic teachings with her," Gloria said.

• 7 •

It Started as a Quick Spin Around the Block, But It Ended with a Visit to the Gardens of Heaven

Ten-year-old Randy Gehling of Arlington Heights, Illinois, had been begging for a new bicycle for his birthday all summer long. On September 8, 1988, the tenth anniversary of his arrival on planet Earth, he got his bicycle—but he also came very close to changing his mailing address to Heaven.

Steve and Kathy Gehling, Randy's parents, found the accident bitterly ironic.

"For months he begs for a new bike for his birthday," Steven said. "The minute he spotted it on the porch, he tore off the ribbons, ignored the eight little friends gathered for his birthday celebration, and took off for a 'quick spin' around the block. He just didn't seem to see the teenager from across the street using the alley as a shortcut home."

Kathy remembered the anguish of the long hours that they spent in the waiting room, not knowing for certain whether their son would live or die.

"He had been unconscious ever since the neighbor boy hit him with his car. His new bicycle was all mangled. Some of the neighbors said that Randy was sent flying fifteen or twenty feet by the impact. All we could do was pray."

After a three-hour surgery, the doctor visited them in the waiting room and told them that the prognosis looked good. Randy was in a recovery room, and as soon as it was advisable, he would be wheeled to a hospital room where they could wait by his bedside. The doctor could not promise whether Randy would be conscious enough to respond to them yet that night.

The next morning at about seven-twenty, about seventeen hours after his accident, Randy opened his eyes, saw his parents at his bedside, and smiled.

He accepted their gentle hugs and kisses in silence, then he told them, "Wow, Mom and Dad, what a trip!"

Steve and Kathy chuckled at their son's first words. Then at a loss for the proper response to such a comment, Steve said, "Yeah, I guess you really went flying over the handlebars, eh?"

Randy nodded, then winced at the pain of the movement. His head was completely swatched in bandages, leaving him with only a peephole around his eyes and a small open space for his mouth. "Yeah, I flew up to the stars and went to Heaven. I saw the angels, and I even think I might have seen Jesus. Oh, and I saw Grandpa Hansen, too."

Steve and Kathy glanced at one another in meaningful silence.

"He's still under the effects of the anesthetic," Kathy whispered. "It's like he's dreaming."

Randy protested what he overheard of his mother's whispered analysis. "It was no dream. I was there!"

Steve and Kathy decided to agree with their son so they would not aggravate his condition so soon after surgery. But over the next few days and weeks, they came to have a different opinion of their ten-year-old son's visit to Heaven. They had to admit that Randy may well have experienced much more than a dream.

According to the notes taken by Kathy Gehling, here, somewhat abbreviated, is Randy's account of his near-death experience:

"I didn't really know what had hit me. I just seemed to go flying through the air.

"And then a really funny thing happened. A part of me—I guess my soul—just kept flying, and I saw my body smash into the ground. I knew it had to hurt to land that hard, so I was happy that I was where I was—wherever that was.

"When I got a little higher, I saw that it had been Kurt's car that had hit me. I always told him that he drove too fast in the neighborhood. He would usually just make a face at me or flip me the bird. He should have listened to me. I figured that he must have killed me and now he would go to jail."

Randy felt a moment of panic when he realized that he might be dying.

"But then this beautiful angel appeared beside me. She was really pretty. She looked like a movie star with wings. Her voice sounded kind of like Mom's when she is comforting me when I have a stomachache or something.

"She told me not to worry. She said that she was with me and that she would stay right by my side. She took my hand, and I felt a lot better."

Randy said that they soon approached a dark tunnel. When he held back and said that he was afraid to go into the darkness, the angel smiled and told him that this was the only way that they could get to their final destination.

"I could see a bright light at the far end of the tunnel, so I said, 'All right, as long as you don't let go of my hand!'

"She laughed and said, 'I told you that I would

never leave your side. I have been with you ever since you were born. In fact, I was there at your mother's side when you were born. I am your guardian angel.' "

Randy asked her what her name was.

"We don't have names in the manner that you mean," she said, "but if it makes you feel better to call me something, you may call me, Areo (ah-ree-o)."

The tunnel did not prove to be such a terrible ordeal after all. Randy and Areo seemed to whoosh through it quickly.

"And then we stood before this totally awesome light," Randy said. "It was so bright and powerful that you really couldn't look right at it.

"I looked at Areo, wondering what we were to do next. She said that we would enter the Light and become One with it. Before I could ask what that meant, she just gave my hand a little tug, and then we were inside the Light.

"That was really cool! I kind of felt as though my body exploded—in a nice way—and became a million different atoms—and each single atom could think its own thoughts and have its own feelings. All at once I seemed to feel like I was a boy, a girl, a dog, a cat, a fish. Then I felt like I was an old man, an old women—and then a little tiny baby."

And then Randy and Areo were standing in what appeared to be a lovely park, bedecked with "millions and millions" of colorful flowers. Randy could hear beautiful music playing somewhere off in the distance.

"Just a little ways off I could see a bridge with someone standing on it. Beyond the bridge, I saw a golden city with towers like European castles. The whole city seemed to be shining with light that shot up into the sky like a giant searchlight.

"I could see that some of the domes of the city were red, others were gold, and a few were blue. The gates and walls of the city seemed to be made of bright blue, red, and violet lights."

Randy asked Areo if they were going to visit the city.

The angel nodded. "That's to be your new home, Randy."

They began walking toward the bridge to the city, and Randy saw that the man standing awaiting them was his Grandpa Hansen.

Randy ran to his grandfather and felt his strong arms close around him. Grandpa Hansen had been a farmer all of his life in Minnesota. He had died, still a powerful man, when Randy was six.

Randy asked his beloved grandfather if he would now be living with him in Heaven.

"One day," Grandpa Hansen told him. "But not just yet."

When Randy questioned his grandfather, he told him that he still had things to learn on

Earth. "You nearly bought the farm this time, Randy-boy," Grandpa Hansen said with a chuckle. "But you aren't ready to cash in your chips just yet."

Aero seemed puzzled. "But it seemed to me that I was doing the right thing. The word that I received indicated that now was Randy's time to return home."

Grandpa Hansen shrugged. "I was told to meet you at the bridge and tell you to take him back home. He's got some lessons that he hasn't learned yet—and lots of work that he hasn't even started to fulfill."

Before Areo took him by the hand for the return flight home, Randy said that another figure materialized beside Grandpa Hansen on the bridge.

"I knew right away that it was Jesus," Randy said, convinced of the majestic visitor. "I knew by his eyes."

Randy couldn't quite remember all of the things that Jesus said, but he is certain of some of the words.

"Jesus said that I would never quite be the same as I was before I visited Heaven. He said that some of the power of the light would remain within me. And he told me to let the love that I would feel in my heart express itself to all people.

"He said that I should never worry if people

doubted my story or could not understand what I was telling them. 'One day,' Jesus said, 'everyone will come to see for themselves what you have seen.' "

• 8 •

The Sleep of the Snows Brought Him to Death's Door

In a classic case from the previous century, Reverend L. J. Bertrand, a Huguenot minister, went on a mountain-climbing vacation in the Alps with a group of his students—and found proof of his lifelong preaching when he experienced the process of the soul's capacity to leave the physical body.

Bertrand's energy advanced him far ahead of the rest of his lagging party. The students accompanying him—their physical ability unable to match their exuberance—straggled behind with the local guide. The clergyman became impatient for them to catch up with him, for they were carrying his lunch.

He found a rock to sit on and he settled

himself down to wait with as much patience as he could muster. Soon after, however, he found himself drifting into the "sleep of the snows." He began to lose all mobility, and he realized with a sudden shock that he was freezing to death.

The fatal freezing process had been gradual and unnoticed, but now Bertrand suddenly felt a moment of intense pain, which he interpreted as the throes of physical death.

When the spasm ended, Bertrand was bobbing above his body as if he were a helium-filled balloon on a silver string. Below him, he could see the near-frozen hulk of his physical body.

The clergyman's thoughts turned toward his students, and immediately he was with them, watching with great annoyance as they repeatedly made wrong turns. He was also horrified with the particularly amateurish climbing methods of most of them.

Bertrand felt a special surge of irritation when he saw the guide duck behind a rock and partake of the very lunch that he was supposed to be bringing to him.

The minister next thought of his wife, who was to join him in Lucerne within three days.

To his astonishment, he perceived her arriving in the Swiss city at that very moment in a carriage with four other travelers. His beloved wife was three days ahead of schedule.

Bertrand continued to hover near her in spirit

form, actually observing her go through the procedure of registering at the hotel.

It was at that time that his laggard students and the local guide came upon his frozen body.

Immediately the guide set about employing the old folk remedy of rubbing Bertrand's body with snow in an effort to stimulate sluggish circulation.

The clergyman's soul, his essential self, however, hovered above the alpine scene on the silver cord, feeling very loath to return to the cold, empty shell that had housed it for so many years.

But the final choice was not that of Reverend Bertrand. Within minutes he was back in his frostbitten body, hearing the guide's sigh of relief and the cheers of his students.

He rose with difficulty to his feet, shuddering at the cold. Then, turning to his students, he scolded them for not following his instructions and for so clumsily missing so many correct turns.

Whispering among themselves, the startled students cast frightened glances at their pastor. What powers of mind did he possess that he could spy on them from a distance?

Bertrand then turned to the hungry guide and thoroughly berated him for having dipped into his lunch uninvited.

The awestruck man stammered his guilt and offered his apologies to "the man who sees everything."

The clergyman nodded, then offered the guide a warm smile of absolution. "Well, the food probably gave you the energy to save my life— and for that, my friend, I shall be everlastingly grateful."

Many hours later, at the base of the mountain, Bertrand's wife experienced amazement when her husband was not surprised by her early arrival. What was more, he went on to describe the carriage in which she had arrived as well as the other four passengers who had accompanied her.

Bertrand himself had no easy explanation for his near-death experience. It sufficed for him that he had been granted a remarkable demonstration of the immortal soul's capacity to survive physical death.

◆ 9 ◆

The Spiritual Essence Within Each of Us

For the past three hundred years, Western science has been fixated upon the concept that everything in the universe is subject to physical laws and exists only in terms of mass and energy—matter being transformed by energy into a variety of conditions and shapes that come into existence only to pass away eventually in time and space.

From time to time, however, highly regarded scientists have protested that such a view of the universe leaves out a very sizeable portion of reality. British philosopher and mathematician Alfred North Whitehead observed that a strictly materialistic approach to life completely ignored the subjective life of humans—or that area of existence which we commonly term the spiritual. It in no way accounted for emotions—the feelings of love between a man and a woman; the magnificent joy upon hearing a Beethoven symphony; the sense of beauty in sighting a rainbow; the inspiration of religious thought. According to the major tenets of Western science, these things are mere transient illusions—things that people imagine for themselves or dream for themselves—while the only true reality consists in the movement of atoms blindly obeying chemical and physical laws.

Professor Charles Hapgood of Keene State College in New Hampshire once remarked upon this lopsided world view during one of our late-night discussions:

"This soulless 'world machine' was created for us three centuries ago by the genius of Descartes, Newton, and their predecessors. It has proved very useful for the development of physical science.

"Whitehead's attempt to construct a philosophy that would include the experience of peoples' inner lives within the framework of 'reality' has apparently made little dent in our contemporary science, which remains rigidly devoted to this seventeenth-century 'world machine.' Everything must still be explained in terms of the physical action of material bodies being acted upon by external forces."

But even the most devout high priests of the

materialistic religion of test tubes, chemical compounds, and mathematical formulas still cannot answer the ultimate question—*what lies beyond physical death?*

The doctrine of immortality is an integral part of all the major world religions, but, admits Professor Hapgood, if a physical scientist is true to his basic principles, he cannot accept it.

"To the physical scientist," Professor Hapgood continued, "if he or she is consistent, life can exist only within a physical frame, a mortal body—and death is the end of the life of the individual.

"Some scientists compromise by accepting both points of view, because their instincts or desires tempt them to hope that life goes on, but they cannot be consistent.

"The consistent materialist has to regard death as the end.

"A good many philosophers have tried to solve this conundrum of mind and matter—which of the two is greater?—but none of them has come any closer than did the old Vermont housewife who quipped, 'What's mind? No matter. What's matter? Never mind!' "

It may be all well and good for some researchers to stop here, but such action does nothing to answer several perplexing questions raised by the phenomenon of near-death experiences, such as, "What is it *within* us that is projected to other dimensions of reality during near-death experiences?

The answers that come to us from those men and women who have experienced NDE are subjective, of course, but they do provide us with valuable clues.

Nearly all of those who have undergone a NDE express an awareness of some type of body image. Many state that they see themselves as "golden bowls" or globular or egg-shaped spheres of some sort, which may eventually assume the more familiar shape of their own physical form. A good many reported cases of near-death refer to the existence of a "silver cord" of great elasticity which appears to connect the spiritual body to the physical body.

Throughout the centuries there has been a rather remarkable consensus regarding the NDE, which seems to have been reached informally by those scholars and metaphysicians who have kept records of such experiences and by those men and women who underwent a NDE at the moment of serious accident, during an illness, in times of extreme exhaustion, or other physical crisis points. The largest body of collected subjective evidence seems to support the description of a spiritual body that is more or less egg-shaped with an orangish glow.

Those of Christian orientation who have undergone the NDE sometimes quote Ecclesiastes 12:5–7 as scriptural testimony to the reality of the spiritual body and its ability to separate itself from the flesh:

"Or ever the silver cord be loosed, or the golden bowl be broken, or the pitcher be broken at the fountain, or the wheel be broken at the cistern. Then shall the dust return to the earth as it was; and the spirit shall return unto God who gave it."

In the early 1970s, I corresponded with the highly respected British marine biologist Sir Alister Hardy, D.Sc., F.R.S., Emeritus Professor at Oxford, who readily conceded that science can no more elucidate the "inner essence" of spirituality than it can the nature of art or the poetry of human love. But he steadfastly maintained that ". . . an organized scientific knowledge— indeed one closely related to psychology— dealing with the records of man's religious experience . . . need not destroy the elements of religion which are most precious to man—any more than our biological knowledge of sex need diminish the passion and beauty of human love."

Sir Alister, an exacting scientist, regarded himself as a "true Darwinian," but he granted that the DNA code that determined the physical nature of an individual might not give us a complete account of the evolution process. The mental, the nonmaterial side of life, he admitted, "turns out to be of cardinal importance within the process of Darwinian evolution."

Contending that spiritual experiences could be subject to scientific scrutiny, Sir Alister generously provided me with data that he had collected for his Religious Experience Research Unit, which he had established at Manchester College in England. Numerous accounts detailed ecstatic transfiguration experiences, the hearing of inspirational voices, feelings of Oneness with the universe, lucid dream experiences, and near-death projections to other dimensions of awareness.

Here, identified by number in order to protect the anonymity of the subjects, are a few representative selections from Sir Alister's files:

(198) "A marvelous beam of spiritual power shot through me, linking me in rapture with the world, the Universe, Life with a capital 'L' All delight and power, all things living, all time fused in a brief second."

(183)"It was as if I were *surrounded by golden light,* and as if I only had to reach out my hand to touch God himself, who was so surrounding me with His compassion."

(712) "It seemed to me that, in some way, I was extending into my surroundings and was becoming one with them. At the same time, I felt a sense of lightness, exhilaration, and power as if I was beginning to understand the true meaning of the whole Universe."

(201) "In the darkness, I cried, 'Oh, God, Oh, God. Please help,' then burst into tears. . . .

From that night onward, a strange calm came over me as I felt the tug of an unseen hand guiding me and leading me to do things I would not otherwise have done."

Sir Alister admitted to me that some people were offended by his attempt to apply the scientific method to something as delicate and sacred as religious experiences. On other occasions he had been scolded for not being satisfied with the evidence of spiritual experience to be found in the Bible and in the works and lives of the mystics and the saints.

"I do not argue that the Scriptures contain profound examples of these kinds of experiences," he said, "but it is also important to demonstrate that these experiences are just as real and as vital to modern individuals as they were in the lives of those of long ago."

As might be expected, Sir Alister did not view God anthropomorphically, as some great father image sitting on a golden throne in Heaven, but he expressed his firm belief in ". . . extrasensory contact with a Power which is *greater than,* and in part lies *beyond the individual self.*"

At the same time that he was catching fire from the offended orthodox religionists for his scientific inquiries into spiritual occurrences, Sir Alister was receiving steady bombardment from certain of his scientific colleagues who held his research in open contempt and had begun to characterize him as a senile old man attempting to carry out some sentimental whim.

Although Sir Alister was seventy-five years old at the time of our correspondence, the ecologist-biologist was quick to answer those who sighed about "poor old Hardy" with the statement that he had long been interested in religion and had been preparing for this monumental study for over twenty-five years.

"A biology based upon an acceptance of the mechanistic hypothesis is a marvelous extension of chemistry and physics," he said, "but to call it an entire science of life is a pretense. I cannot help feeling that much of man's unrest today is due to the widespread intellectual acceptance of this mechanistic superstition when the common sense of his intuition cries out that it is false."

Sir John Eccles is another highly esteemed scientist who has declared that evolution alone cannot explain our awareness of ourselves. Winner of the Nobel Prize for medicine in 1963, Sir John is the complete scientist, philosopher, and metaphysician. As the scientist who demonstrated his transmission of electrical impulses in the brain, he is well-acquainted with the workings of humankind's mental machinery, and he has become increasingly convinced that there must have been the intervention of some transcendental agency in the infusion into humankind of Soul.

Simply stated, he maintains that the brain and the mind are separate entities which interact, but it is only the brain that is the product of genetic evolution.

In an interview with Sandy Rovner of the *Washington Post* (April, 1981), Sir John explained his hypothesis in this way:

"I am an evolutionist, of course, but I don't believe that evolution is the final story. . . .

"The genetic code and natural selection explain quite a lot, but evolution doesn't explain . . . the evolution of consciousness. . . . If you look at the most modern texts on evolution, you find nothing about mind and consciousness. They assume that it just comes automatically with the development of the brain. But that's not an answer.

"If my uniqueness of self is tied to the genetic uniqueness of self that built my brain, the odds against myself existing are ten to the ten-thousandth against.

"It is just too improbable to wait around to get the right constructed brain for you. The brain is a computer, you see. Each of us has a computer, and we are the programmers of this computer. [We were] born . . . with what this wonderful structure of evolution and genetic coding have wrought. . . .

"But the soul is this unique creation that is ours for life. It is us. We are experiencing, remembering, creating, suffering, imagining. All of this is processed here with the soul central to it."

Dr. Robert Crookall, a British biologist and botanist, was one of the great pioneers in the clinical study of near-death and out-of-body experiences. In 1969, he did me the great honor of recognizing some of my early work in the field by initiating a correspondence with me and by sending me a number of his books and papers on the subject. I had only recently begun distributing the Steiger Questionnaire of Mystical, Paranormal, and UFO experiences, and I was enormously pleased that Dr. Crookall had looked with favor on my efforts.

Dr. Crookall theorized that what metaphysicians had labeled the astral or the etheric body—the soul—is normally "enmeshed in" or "in gear" with the familiar physical body so that most people are never aware of its existence.

"But many people have become aware of [the Soul Body], for with them [during out-of-body and near-death experiences] the Soul Body separated or projected from the physical body and was used, temporarily, as an instrument of consciousness."

According to Dr. Crookall, this "Soul Body" consists of matter, ". . . but it is extremely subtle and may be described as 'superphysical.' "

Dr. Crookhall perceived the physical body as animated by a semiphysical "vehicle of vitality," which serves as a bridge between the physical body and the Soul Body. This, he believed, was the "breath of life" mentioned in Genesis.

In some people, he speculated, ". . . especially (though not necessarily) saintly people," the Soul Body may be less confined to the physical flesh than it is in persons of a more sensual nature, thus making it easier for the aesthetic to achieve out-of-body experiences.

"With some very few people," Dr. Crookhall theorized, "and these may be either saintly or sensual, the vehicle of vitality is loosely associated with the physical body, and it may readily project part of its substance."

As we have mentioned previously, in the literature of near-death and out-of-body experiences there are many references to a psychic "umbilical cord" that appears to connect the nonphysical Soul Body to the physical body. Dr. Crookall cited many from his own research:

"With regard to *form*, several . . . have described seeing merely a 'cord' (and said it was about half an inch wide). T.D. compared his to a 'thread.' H. considered, 'I am sure that, had a *feeble thread* between soul and body been severed, I would have remained intact' (*i.e.*, the soul would have survived the death of the body).

"The Tibetans also observed that 'a strand' subsisted between the [Soul Body] and the [physical] body.

"Like H. (and Ecclesiastes), Miss K. realized

that once [the cord] was 'loosed' the reentry . . . into the body would have been impossible. She said, 'This is what death means.'"

One oft-observed quality of the silver cord which connects the Soul Body to the physical body is its elasticity. Countless persons who have undergone near-death experiences have remarked upon this quality in their descriptions of the experience.

Dr. Crookhall wrote of a man named Edwards who stated that from the pull of his silver cord he would characterize it as being made of a some kind of substance similar to "stout elastic."

Another of Dr. Crookall's subjects, a Mrs. Leonard, noted that as her Soul Body neared her physical body, the cord not only became "shorter and thicker," as would be expected, but also "less elastic," agreeing with the oft-reported statements that when the Soul Body approaches very near the physical body, it tends to reenter it—in fact, it is often "sucked" back.

And what of our spiritual essence when we *do* make the *final projection?*

George S. Arundale in his *Nirvana* wrote: "There is no death, only change—and always change with a greater purpose, change to a greater end.

"Death is re-creation, renewal, the dropping of fetters, the casting aside of a vehicle which has ceased to suffice.

"Death is, in very truth, a birth into a fuller and larger life—or a dipping down into matter under the law of readjustment. Progress always, and progress toward Unity. We come ever nearer to each other and to the Real through death."

Dr. Bruce Goldberg, president of the Los Angeles Academy of Clinical Hypnosis, stated recently that near-death experiences confirm the existence of a soul and demonstrate that death is definitely not to be feared.

Dr. Antonino Aldo Soldaro, chief surgeon at Rome's main public hospital and a professor of surgery at Rome University, has observed that all NDE subjects "improve their spiritual and social lives. They become more generous, optimistic, and positive."

A consensus among researchers yields a number of common features described by those who have undergone NDE:

- Moving down what appears to be a tunnel toward a white light.
- Experiencing confusion as to what is happening and frustration at being unable to gain the attention of the living.
- Being met by deceased friends and relatives.
- Encountering an angel, guide, or spirit being who arrives to comfort and to instruct.
- Experiencing a brilliant light.
- Finding themselves in a beautiful paradise.
- Discovering that their consciousness had ex-

panded far beyond that which it was during their mortal lives.

- Experiencing an unwillingness to leave the postmortem state and return to their physical bodies.

• 10 •

A Conversation with an Angel of Light

Recently, one of my correspondents who had filled out his responses to the Steiger Questionnaire of Mystical, Paranormal, and UFO Experiences, provided our files with a detailed account of his near-death experience when he was severely injured after an explosion in the chemistry laboratory in which he is employed.

Jack Ausman had always prided himself on being a solid materialist, a practitioner of pure science. Until his near-death experience, he said bluntly, he would not have approached a book that discussed spiritual matters ". . . with the proverbial ten-foot pole." When he sent for the questionnaire after reading one of our books, he admitted that his universe "was a great deal larger than it had been before his near-fatal accident."

According to Jack, he remembered nothing after one of his coworkers in the laboratory managed to shout a brief exclamation of warning before the explosion shattered the building.

"I was astonished when I saw what appeared to be the traditional representation of an angel flying off with what looked as though it might be Peter, my lab partner.

"And then I was even more astonished when I saw that I—or some part of me—was also being borne aloft by someone or something in what appeared to be a gown of shimmering white. 'Absurd!' I thought. 'I don't even believe in such things!'

"It didn't seem to matter. And it certainly didn't seem to matter what my thoughts were to the silent entity that was bearing me toward a dark tunnel.

"I remember seeing a bright light, feeling a kind of almost sensual, ecstatic sensation—and then I was seated near a lovely forest stream on what appeared to be a marble bench. The tall, imposing angelic figure was seating beside me."

Jack asked if he might inquire exactly what was going on.

The angel shrugged, then smiled warmly. "Don't you think it is rather evident, Jack? Look around you. As you might say, 'This isn't Kansas.'

"Oh, yeah," Jack snapped back. "Well, if you're supposed to be an angel, where are your wings?"

"If you want wings, you'll get wings. I didn't think such traditional trappings would appeal to a disciple of science such as yourself," the angel replied.

"Forget the wings. The white robe is enough."

"If you prefer a business suit, I can arrange it with but a moment's thought."

"Let's stay with the robe."

Jack wrote in his report of the experience that he was surprised to find that his angel had a rather sharp wit. He was not at all pompous or overtly holy.

"Well, in some sense, I am the nonphysical aspect of yourself," the angel told him. "But it is now my task to expand your consciousness and to help you attain a better balance before you return to your body."

"You mean," Jack wanted to know at once, "that I am not dead?"

"Well, you are going to have to cut down on contact sports for a while," the angel replied, "but you will live. We've more or less taken advantage of the accident to get you apart so that we can set you back on the path with greater equilibrium."

Jack pointed out that the angel continued to make references to his being "out of balance."

Just what was it, he wanted to know, that he was doing that was so wrong?

The angel sighed, as if he were a teacher who had just realized that he was stuck with a pupil who was not especially bright. "You've emphasized your intellect to the exclusion of your emotions and your spiritual growth. If you are to fulfill your true mission on Earth, you must recognize the importance of the nonphysical aspects of existence."

Jack wanted to know if that was typical "angel work"?

"For centuries now," the angel answered. "It seems that not many humans are given to know the truth of things. So it has been down through the ages of Earth. Yet we look forward and foresee a world of humans living in a greater vibration of the Light than exists on Earth today.

"In that glorious day to come, Earth men and women will see and understand how near we of the heavenly kingdom are to them. Meanwhile, we do our part, ever watchful, ever hopeful—and if our heavenly joy is often mixed with sadness, it is because we cannot yet walk hand-in-hand with you on Earth. Still again, we know that we are coming closer and closer together—and all is working according to the great Divine Plan."

The angel smiled at him, and Jack was certain that he had seen his face somewhere before.

"Perhaps in dreams," the being acknowledged. "And certainly when you were a small body. You are my ward, you see; so let us take advantage of these current conditions for me to present certain teachings for you to take back with you.

"While we are pleased that you work with Earth sciences, we want to instruct you to explore deeper into those fundamentals that are of a spiritual origin. Worldly science is only beginning to acknowledge the unseen realms. If your science would put more emphasis on the nonmaterial aspects of existence, then our two worlds would be able to draw closer together.

"One thing that humans must keep in mind: the Universe was not created for them alone—any more than the sea was created for the use of one particular fish or the air was created for the pleasure of one particular bird.

"The human entity invades both sea and air and calls them his own kingdoms to conquer and to use—and to a certain extent, he is correct. These kingdoms do not belong to the birds or to the fish. Dominion is given to the greater being—and that being is humankind. Humans, by permission, rule Earth and the dominion over which their Maker has placed them.

"But there are beings greater than humankind; and as humans rule the lesser entities and use them for the development of their faculties and personality, so do the greater beings rule humankind and use them.

"And this process is just and wise, for the angels, archangels, and princes and powers of God are His servants also, and their development and training is as necessary as those of humankind. But by how much these entities are greater than humankind, respectively, so must the means and the material of their training be of a higher nature and of a more sublime nature. According to the innate power of any being—human or angel—so is his or her environment proportioned and constituted.

"If humans kept the hierarchy of beings more clearly in mind, then they would better appreciate the gift of free will that has been given to them. And be assured that this gift is one that no one of the heavenly hierarchy may ever take from humankind. And they would not if they could, for by so doing their own substance would be deteriorated in quality and they would become less capable of their own advancement. Humans are, and must ever remain, beings of free will."

Jack had many questions, but each time that he made a sound or movement that signaled an interruption, the angel silenced him with a glance.

"I soon came to understand," Jack said, "that my angelic teacher was very much aware of our limitations of time and that he wished to make the best use of our moments together."

The angel next explained that the one great

power that animated all those who served the Living Creator God in the heavenly dimension was that of Divine Love.

"In this dimension," Jack's celestial tutor said, "power means an issuing forth of love—and the greater the power, the greater the love which is sent forth.

"When you return to Earth, my ward, see to it that your work becomes one with our own. We have only one object set before us—the betterment of all life and all things. We follow this, our mission, with humility and simple trust in Divine Love. And we take great delight in assisting all human entities who become our fellow workers in the one great assignment in the universe of the Living God.

"Do not become discouraged. From our perspective, we see far more than you human entities of the effects of evil—war, murder, rape, poverty, so-called 'genetic cleansings,' exploitation of the weak. And yet we do not despair, because we are able to see more clearly the meaning and the purpose of all these things. And thus seeing, we know that humankind will one day ascend to the higher spheres of service and from this point of higher elevation continue its evolution as spiritual beings.

"Remember the words of the Prince of Peace: 'To him that overcometh will I give to sit with Me in My Throne, even as I overcame and am set down with My Father in His Throne.'

"To the strong who overcome is the Kingdom, my dear ward; and now our session must come to an end. It is time for you to return to your physical body.

"Do well, and you shall fare well. God's light will be around you, and you shall not stumble."

Jack concluded his account by stating that he had been badly burned and injured in the laboratory fire. He had been unconscious for two days, and for several hours, the attending physicians did not expect him to live. His laboratory partner, Peter, had been killed outright by the blast.

"I am now a very different person," he said. "My wife and my children take delight in this, for I now take much more time to 'smell the roses.' I am less of a workaholic.

"I like to think, as my angel advised me, that I have become a much more balanced individual, acknowledging both the physical and nonphysical aspects of reality—and I see no conflict in serving both facets of the universe."

• 11 •

His Near-Death Experience Summoned a Spirit Teacher Who Instructed Him to Keep Only Love in His Heart

"I thought I was dead for certain that night when that automobile struck mine at the intersection in my hometown of Nogales, Arizona," Ernest Martinez wrote in the letter that accompanied his questionnaire.

"What seemed to be the *real me* was somewhere above the wreck looking down on all the confusion. I watched the other driver get out of his car and shake his head, as if he were dazed by the blow. Other than a cut on his forehead, he seemed all right. I saw the police and a crowd arrive, and I could see my bleeding body slumped forward against the steering wheel. 'This is it,' I thought. 'I am really dead.'

"I wanted to see my wife Laura one last time.

Then I discovered that all I had to do was to form the thought—and I was there beside her. I watched her fixing our dinner. She was, of course, completely unaware of either the accident or my spirit body there beside her.

"I thought of my only child, my son Edward from my first marriage. In an instant I was bobbing above him in my spirit body, observing him as he sat at his desk in his office in Phoenix.

"I felt no real sorrow at leaving Laura and Edward, but I was thankful that I was somehow given the opportunity to see them one last time."

It was at that point that Ernest felt something tugging at his right hand.

"I should really say my 'right side,' as I didn't really seem to be any longer in human form. I actually looked more like a kind of egg yolk floating above the physical 'me' in the car below."

The "something" that was tugging at him appeared to be either an angel or one of the saints.

"He didn't have wings, and he was dressed in a long, flowing robe. He had a full beard and long, shoulder-length hair. I suppose he could have been St. Peter, but we never got as far as the gates of Heaven."

Ernest remembered that the two of them seemed to be sitting in some kind of room, "kind of like a waiting room in a doctor's office."

The spiritual guide—whoever he might have been—was very direct in his words to Ernest.

"Now you understand why you must not carry hatred in your heart," he said in a low, rumbling bass voice. "You never know when your life is going to be taken from you; and if you harbor hatred, such negative energy weighs heavily upon your soul."

Ernest knew at once that the saintly figure was referring to an animosity which he felt toward one of his coworkers in the office. He was certain that the man had deliberately lied about him to their boss and had cost him an important promotion. Ernest had cursed the man to his face, even threatened him in the parking lot. He had told Laura that he would get even with the man if it took him the rest of his life.

Now, it appeared that his life was over, and the hatred he bore the man was weighing his soul down. Maybe even to Hell!

"As a churchgoing man, you have heard often of the unconditional love of Jesus for his enemies," the being said. "Like so many other men, you have marveled at this aspect of Divine Love, the ability to forgive one's enemies.

"Jesus' first commandment to his human flock was that they love one another. This is the greatest commandment—and the hardest for humans to keep. People always agree in moments of quiet and peace that to love one another is good. But when it comes time to translate that sentiment into action, how they sadly fail.

"And yet, my son," the bearded teacher continued, "without love nothing in all the universe could stand. Without love, everything would fall into decay and dissolution.

"Humans must realize that it is the love of God that energizes all that is. You will be able to see the fruits of God's Divine Love everywhere— once you learn to look for it.

"When one man hates another, he is likely to cease being able to love anyone as completely as he should. The larger the hatred grows, the more difficult it becomes to love anything at all.

"The human propensity toward hatred is one of the most difficult things to overcome for your advancement toward the heavenly realms," the entity said. "Not until a human has learned to love all others without hating anyone is he or she able to progress toward the Light. In this higher sphere, my son, love is light, and light is love. Those who do not love must move in dark places where they are apt to lose their way completely.

"My son, just as you think of God with reverence, awe, and love, so you must think of your fellow humans with reverence, respect, and love. Do this, knowing that we of the heavenly realms are watching you and steadily charting your progress toward the spiritual kingdom. Understand that we mark down with precision the workings of your inner mind. As you are on Earth, so will you be when you are awakened here for your final and ultimate projection from the physical body."

With that statement, Ernest was led to understand that he was not yet dead.

"Thank you . . . sir," he said to the heavenly being. "I am sorry that I reacted in such an uncharitable and un-Christian way toward my fellow worker. I promise that I will make amends and that I will do my very best never again to harbor such hatred in my heart."

The bearded one nodded knowingly at him—and then Ernest felt a tugging and a pulling sensation.

"I was being literally sucked back into my physical body. I perceived a brilliant, swirling blur of color—and I landed in my body with a spasmodic jerking of my muscles.

"Jeez, doc," he heard someone ask with a chuckle, "what was in that needle? It really snapped him back to life."

Ernest heard another man laugh, and then he opened his eyes to see what appeared to be a dozen or more people pressing forward to view the accident scene.

"I caught a glimpse of the back of a police officer herding the curiosity seekers back from my car, then a sickening rush of pain caused me to lapse back into unconsciousness," he said in his report of the near-death experience. "This time I went on no out-of-body journey, met no bearded teacher in outer space, and received no further admonishments. when I awakened several hours later in a hospital, my wife Laura was holding my hand."

Ernest did add a meaningful postscript to his account.

"A couple of weeks later, when I was back at work, I did some checking and learned that I had wrongfully accused my coworker of having bad-mouthed me to the boss. I offered my sincere apologies—and thank Heaven, he accepted them. We have since become good friends.

"I thank God every day that I was given another chance to come back to life, and I am going to work very hard at keeping my record book clean—and my heart clear of hatred."

· 12 ·

"My Soul Left My Body Like a Silk Handkerchief Being Pulled from a Pocket"

It was August 23, 1944, and an armored-car officer was riding in a car that was transporting explosives to the frontlines. Within minutes, the officer was to experience a demonstration of the Great Mystery that would prove to him the survival of the soul after death.

The armored car was hit directly by a German antitank gun, and the explosive cargo it carried split the car apart like a rotten log. The officer himself was flung nearly twenty-five feet from the car and over a five-foot hedge.

"I was conscious of being two persons—one lying on the ground in a field where I had fallen from the blast, my clothes on fire, waving my limbs about wildly, at the same time uttering moans and gibbering with fear," the officer wrote later in a report for the *Journal of the Society for Psychical Research*, Volume 34. "The other 'me' was floating up in the air, about twenty feet from the ground, from which position I could see not only my other self on the ground, but also the hedge, the road, and the car, which was surrounded by smoke and burning fiercely."

The officer's essential self, his soul, told the physical body that it was useless to thrash about and babble. With an effort of will, he impressed upon his body that it should roll over and over until the flames were smothered and put out.

Then, like a marionette, its strings controlled from above by the officer's Real Self, the body rolled over and over until it fell into a puddle of water in a ditch beneath the hedge. The flames were extinguished and, at that moment, the officer and his body became one again.

"Perhaps the aerial viewpoint might be explained up to a point as a 'photograph' taken subconsciously as I was passing over the hedge as a result of the blast," the officer theorized. "This, however, does *not* explain the fact that I saw 'myself' quite clearly on the ground and for what seemed like a long time—though it could not have been more than a minute or so."

No experience is ever lost on a writer. Everything that happens to him or her becomes grist for the creative mill. Author Ernest Hemingway had a near-death experience while serving in the trenches near Fossalta, Spain. It was July 18, 1918 when the nineteen-year-old Hemingway was badly wounded in the legs by a mortar shell exploding nearby.

Some years later, the author told Guy Hickok, a European correspondent for the Brooklyn *Daily Eagle*, that he had experienced death at that moment. Hemingway said that he had felt his soul coming out of his body ". . . like you'd pull a silk handkerchief out of a pocket by one corner. It /his soul/ flew around and then came back and went in again, and I wasn't dead anymore."

Hemingway made use of his own personal near-death experience in his novel *A Farewell to Arms* when his fictional hero Frederick Henry underwent the same sensations.

Henry is positioned in the Italian trenches when ". . . a blast furnace door is swung open, and a roar that started white and went red and on and on in rushing wind." He feels his essence rush out of himself and soar with the wind. He believes himself to be dead and realizes that there is an existence beyond physical death.

Then ". . . instead of going on, I felt myself slide back. I breathed and I was back."

• 13 •

The Spirit of a Deceased Friend Guided Her Back to Life

In October of 1980, Mrs. Cynthia Chapman of Plymouth, England, underwent two very serious operations. As she was regaining consciousness the morning after her second visit to the operating room, she remembers lying in bed listening to her heart "pounding like a dynamo."

Then she felt herself slipping away into a pool of darkness. She seemed to be tumbling, turning over and over—and then she found herself no longer lying in a hospital bed, but standing at the doorway to a vast gray hall.

"In front of the doorway was a beautiful light that seemed to lead me through the portal and into a large room that appeared to be some kind of library," Cynthia said. "Seated at a great desk was a figure dressed in long, flowing silvery robes."

At first Cynthia was frightened of the figure, for its face was hidden in shadows caused by a cowl that hooded its features.

"I figured that I must have died and gone to some kind of place of judgment," she said. "It seemed as though the hooded figure was sitting there surrounded by books that had recorded the good deeds and the misdeeds of everyone. I started to think that this was the angel that had been assigned to my case to jot down every single one of my missteps. I knew that I hadn't been some evil monster, but I also knew that I hadn't been any angel."

A beam of light suddenly emanated from the entity, and Cynthia began to relax.

"It now occurred to me that I was supposed to approach the hooded figure and be guided into the light. The entity really was my guardian angel and it would help me become one with the light."

Then, to her frustration, each time she tried to move forward toward the hooded entity in the flowing silvery robes, she could feel something holding her back.

"I wanted to cry in despair," Cynthia said, "for I now desired so much to reach the hooded angel.

"But then I felt the presence of a friend near me. I turned around and looked into the smiling face of David Miller, an old boyfriend who had died in an automobile accident five years before. As soon as I saw David, I felt warm and comforted."

"Hey, Cyn," David said with a grin, "you don't want to go in there yet, girl. You don't want to have any dealing with that gent for many years yet. It's time for you to go back home now."

Cynthia glanced back at the hooded figure, and she no longer felt a great yearning to reach it.

"The entity stood up, and the cowl fell away from its face. I could see that it was a man with long white hair and that he was smiling at me."

"He's a patient one, he is," David told me. "He'll wait until it's your time for sure."

When Cynthia turned back to speak to her friend, she found that he had vanished.

"Then I felt myself floating back to my body. I felt a great peace and quiet come over me. I knew that I was going to get better."

A hospital spokesperson later admitted to Cynthia that they had nearly lost her because of her loss of blood and the strain on her system.

"I amazed the staff by recovering ahead of the schedule that they had projected for me," she said, "but I now feel that I know what death really means—and I no longer fear it."

Cynthia Chapman is convinced that if she had

been able to reach the cowled figure in the great library she would have died.

"When the spirit form of my friend David came along, however, I knew that I must return to my body and to life.

"I must admit, though," she said, "I wanted to stay there and not return. But like David said, that old spirit gentleman who keeps records is a patient one. He'll be waiting there for me one day. The thing of it is, I now know that death is nothing to fear."

From Death on the Delivery Table to "The Most Beautiful Place" She Had Ever Seen

Mrs. Josephine Hand received her profound belief in an afterlife when she lay on the delivery table in a Georgia hospital, officially diagnosed as dead.

Complications had soon developed when she was admitted to the hospital on January 16, 1965, and the unfortunate woman suffered a day and night of excruciating labor pains.

"The pain was so terrible that I lost consciousness several times," she related. "When it came time for me to deliver, I was in a state of shock. I had lost touch with reality and had become unconscious."

Then, according to Josephine, she was "... floating through space in the most beautiful place I have ever seen. Two beautiful white wings trimmed in gold appeared on my back, and I remember feeling free and thinking what a wonderful sensation I was experiencing."

Her doctor later told her that she had stopped breathing, and anxious medical attendants could find no heartbeat. Clinically, she was dead; but her doctor worked feverishly to reverse the cruel verdict. Desperately he and his staff tried every procedure they could think of to bring the deceased woman back to life. They had just delivered a healthy baby son. It would be a tragedy if they were to lose the mother.

"My doctor told me that they had fought for nearly thirteen minutes to save my life," Josephine said, "but all I remember is floating into eternity."

"I recall drifting down a long, dark tunnel that seemed to stretch ahead of me for miles and miles. Finally, I reached its end."

Later, when she was asked about her impressions of the long tunnel and the effect that it had upon her, Josephine replied that she soon realized that she was somewhere in "the beautiful hereafter."

"I felt absolutely and completely comfortable. I think I probably felt very much like the astronauts feel when they are floating in space."

Josephine went on to state that she had an awareness of herself dressed in what appeared to be a long, white shroud with sleeves that covered her hands and flowed beneath her bare feet.

In her particular case, she did not recall seeing any other spirit, entities, angels, or holy figures.

"When I floated out of the dark tunnel, I was in an open area with blue skies and white clouds, and everything around me was beautiful beyond description," she said. "When I regained complete consciousness, I was in an oxygen tent, and the nurse told me that I had given birth to a fine baby son."

Both mother and child remained for several days in the hospital, thus allowing Josephine ample time to recover from the tremendous strain under which her system had been placed. It was during this time that she was informed by her physician of her technical death.

Josephine Hand has repeatedly stated that she considered her near-death experience to have been a "wonderful" occurrence. "I am grateful that I was given an opportunity to get a good look at the next life, but I thank God for sparing me and for letting me come back so that I could take care of my son."

• 15 •

"I Shall Never Again Fear Death!"

It was Christmas morning, 1957, and Mrs. Oleta A. Martin was up early straightening the house for her children, who had arrived with their families for a holiday dinner.

The temptingly tasty aroma of the cooking turkey was beginning to permeate the entire house as Oleta scrutinized the dining room once more for anything that might be out of order. She did so like the house to be in perfect order when the children and grandchildren visited.

All at once she was seized with a pain in her heart that dangerously constricted her breathing—so much so that she could not even call for help.

Oleta's youngest daughter entered the room,

took one look at her stricken mother, and ran upstairs to awaken the rest of the sleeping family.

Her husband moved her to a sofa, and the entire family stood by, helplessly watching the woman in her excruciating pain. Someone went to call for a doctor.

Oleta's eyes closed, and she thought that she must be dying.

She seemed to be floating away. She had lost all sense of pain and all consciousness of her surroundings.

When she stopped floating, she found herself at the edge of a wide chasm, "so dark beneath me . . . I could not see the bottom."

She experienced a great fear, then calm, when a bright "spiritual" light appeared on the other side of the abyss.

Oleta could make out the general form of a being in the midst of the light, but the illumination surrounding the entity was so brilliant that she could see no part of him from his shoulders up.

To the being's left stood a dozen or so other beings in long, white garments. They all seemed to be telling her not to be afraid, that she could cross the chasm without danger and that they would be waiting for her on the other side.

Oleta was eager to join them, but the awareness was heavy upon her that once she crossed that wide chasm, she might never be able to return. She thought of how she would miss her family and how greatly her daughter needed her just now.

"The pressure on my chest returned," Oleta Martin wrote in the June 1969 issue of *Fate* magazine. "I gasped for breath and again became conscious of the world around me.

"I opened my eyes to see my family's tears change to surprise as they saw that I smiled weakly."

Oleta's assembled family cried, "Mother!" and moved toward her as one, but the family doctor held them back with a warning that she had just had a close call and must not be excited.

Oleta A. Martin later improved her heart condition with rest, medication, and a change of diet, but she writes: ". . . when the time does come I shall be less afraid to die because of that memorable experience at the brink of death."

• 16 •

Help from Spirit Guides in Another Dimension

Percy Cole of Melbourne, Australia, sent psychical researchers Hereward Carrington and Sylvan Muldoon a most intriguing case of a near-death experience while he was having some teeth extracted.

Cole's out-of-body experience was preceded by a dream in which he had seen a doctor and a nun dressed in army uniforms. Cole, a pharmacist, sensed that the nun was handing him a prescription, but he was unable to read it. When he looked to the doctor for clarification, the physician told him that the prescription meant that he suffered from "mitral regurgitation."

When Cole awakened, he could not shake the memory of the strange dream from his mind.

The more he thought about it, the more he interpreted the appearance of the nun and the doctor as symbols of warning concerning his approaching dental surgery. He had already scheduled an appointment with a dentist to have several teeth extracted, but now he decided it would be wise to undergo a complete physical examination before he reported for the operation.

Although he had been visiting the same medical doctor for years and normally would have made an appointment with his regular physician, Cole found himself for some unknown reason mounting the steps to the office of a doctor named Bender.

Dr. Bender examined Cole thoroughly and informed him that he had located a slight heart murmur. "Nothing serious, though," the doctor assured him. "Nothing to be concerned about."

In spite of Dr. Bender's assurances, Cole felt uneasy about the discovery of even a mild health condition. He informed the physician of his impending dental surgery, and he asked if Dr. Bender would administer the anesthetic. Dr. Bender agreed, and the operation was scheduled when convenient for all parties.

Three weeks later, Cole lay on the operating table while Dr. Bender stood by with the anesthetic. Dr. H. N. Johnson, the dental surgeon, indicated his readiness, and the procedure was initiated. At first, Cole felt himself fighting the anesthetic, then, finally, he let himself go.

The next thing he knew, Cole wrote in his account of the experience, "I was standing in the corner of the room, near the doorway, with two other people whom I at once recognized."

One was the nun, the other was the doctor, Cole said, but this time he was not dreaming. He could see his physical body lying on the operating table, and as is so often reported in these cases, he experienced no particular identification with it. The doctor and the dentist were engrossed in their work, completely oblivious to the presence of Cole's spirit form or the manifestation of the two entities.

Cole turned his attention to the nun as she began to speak to him, severely berating him for having submitted to a general anesthetic: *"We appeared before you in a dream to warn you that you have mitral regurgitation. Why did you choose to ignore us?"*

In defense of his actions, Cole pointed out that he had gone to see Dr. Bender, who had told him that his heart suffered from only a slight murmur.

"We sent you to Dr. Bender," the nun told him. "Dr. Bender is a man of immense physical vitality—which we are drawing upon at this very moment to keep you alive!

"If you had asked your regular doctor to administer the anesthetic, quite frankly, you would have had no chance to survive this surgery. Your regular doctor is much too fragile."

The spirit doctor spoke next: "Your heart trouble is masked. We had hoped that Dr. Bender would have discovered the full extent of your difficulties, but it was too late. What the sister says is true. Dr. Bender's strength is now required to pull you through this surgery. With your regular doctor, there would have been no doubt of the outcome."

Cole reported the same emotions and feelings toward his physical body as are so often expressed in case studies of near-death experiences.

"I had no feeling of alarm, but was quite calm and detached.

"I could 'hear' the thoughts of the doctor and dentist before they were actually spoken, so that their spoken words seemed like echoes."

Cole was bemused that as the surgery got under way, both medical men were discussing real-estate values.

Things progressed normally for quite some time—and then Cole observed Dr. Bender undergo a moment or two of panic. As he followed the doctor's anxious concern, he saw that he had stopped breathing!

"I cannot explain how I did it," Cole said, "but somehow I managed to make my chest lift in my physical body."

It was at that point that the nun told him that he would have to return to his physical body.

"We have done all we can do for you," she said. "You will have to fight for yourself now."

Cole looked around him and perceived a bright light to his left. On his right he saw a dark tunnel with swirling shadows and a small light at its end.

"Instinctively, I began to struggle for the dark tunnel," Cole said. "Shadows rushed past me, and it seemed a long time before I managed to reach the light at its end. Then I was physically awake again."

While recovering from his near-fatal operation, Cole had the opportunity to question both doctors about their conversation and the events that transpired during the surgery. Both registered surprise at his accurate reporting, and they said that Cole had repeated their dialogue almost word for word. He also detailed in precise manner the order of events surrounding his surgery, though he had been under the full effects of the general anesthetic.

It was not until some months later, however, that Cole was able to see a prominent heart specialist. Under his thorough examination it was discovered that the irregular beat of Cole's heart was masked by a portion of his lung, which overlapped it.

"This, at least partially, confirmed what the spirit nun told me while I was out of the body," Cole concluded.

• 17 •

A Meeting with St. Peter

    "I was crossing a neighbor's driveway near my home about 9:15 P.M. on the evening of September 10, 1987," began Mrs. Evelyn Lovell as she recounted her near-brush with death. "Suddenly I saw two lights coming at me. That was the last thing that I was to see in this physical world for seven weeks."

Evelyn Lovell spent those seven weeks in a deep coma—a sleep from which medical science could not rouse her—and in a lovely region in some other dimension of being. At some point during her long sojourn, Evelyn is convinced that she met St. Peter at the gates of Heaven.

"For what seemed like days, I was floating in some kind of mist," she said. "After just kind of bobbing around in this nebulous state, I finally saw a light off in the distance. I somehow directed myself to float toward the light, but then I saw that it was at the end of a tunnel."

Although she was apprehensive about entering the tunnel, Evelyn was convinced that she wanted to approach nearer to the light. "It seemed important to me to come to the light, to become one with the light."

The instant she entered the tunnel, her spiritual body began to spin and twist at a very rapid pace.

"In what seemed less than a few seconds, I was somehow moving through the light. I felt as though I was being energized by all the love in the universe. It was a feeling of ecstasy beyond anything that could ever be dreamed of on the physical plane."

The next thing that Evelyn knew, she was more or less floating near beautiful orchards and happy, cheery men and women were harvesting basketfuls of rich, ripe fruit.

"After a while, I noticed this very peculiar thing—off to my right was a white stairway and a woman sitting at a desk at its foot."

Evelyn peered closely at the lady behind the desk and realized with a start that it was Denise Matthews, a friend with whom she had gone to high school.

After exchanging warm greetings, Evelyn was

about to ask her friend what she was doing in this lovely orchard.

"And then I caught myself. I dimly recalled the lights bearing down on me in our neighbor's driveway. It finally occurred to me that I had to be dead—and that this place was somewhere on the other side. So that meant that Denise . . ."

As if her friend could hear her every thought, she smiled and nodded her head. "Yes, of course, Evie," Denise said. "You remember that I died seven years ago when I was giving birth to Tommy. You came to my funeral. Remember?"

Evelyn acknowledged her gradual recollection of Denise's death and burial.

"Take this card, hon," Denise told her, handing her what appeared to be something similar to a library card, "and go up those stairs to a gate. I'll see you later."

Evelyn hesitated. Somehow on some intuitive level, she understood that once she walked up those stairs, she would be entering a dimension from which she was not likely to return. She thought of her two small children—Alice and Kirk—and felt a sharp stab of pain and sorrow. She really did not wish to leave her children so young.

But then, she wondered wryly, did anyone ever have a choice as to the time of their demise?

A man was coming in from the orchard whom Evelyn recognized was her uncle Mel Jennings, who had died in 1975.

"Don't be scared to walk those stairs, honey," he told her, offering her his arm. "I'll escort you right up to the top."

Evelyn was astonished to look once again into the blue, twinkling eyes that she had always loved so much. Uncle Mel had been one of her favorite relatives, and she had taken his death very hard.

"All the way to the top of the stairs, we laughed and joked. Uncle Mel asked me about my mom, his sister, and about a lot of his old friends, who he said would soon be joining him in the orchard."

At the top of the stairs, just before the gate, Evelyn and Uncle Mel were met by her maternal grandfather, Bill Jennings, who had died in 1960. Behind her grandfather, according to Uncle Mel, was her great-grandfather, Robert Jennings.

"I figured this really had to be death, what with all my deceased relatives welcoming me to Heaven," Evelyn said. "Behind my great-grandfather, I could see a whole group of folks that I assumed were people on my ancestral tree. A good-sized welcoming committee had certainly turned out in my honor."

The gate slowly opened to admit her, and Evelyn saw standing majestically before her a very elderly man with long white hair and a full, flowing white beard.

"Although he did not identify himself," Evelyn admitted, "I recognized him at once on some deeper level of knowing. He wore beautiful white silky robes, and he was so commanding in appearance that I knew at once that it was St. Peter."

Evelyn handed her card to "St. Peter," the card that Denise had given her at the bottom of the white stairs.

The majestic bearded entity in the magnificent robes took the card, looked at it carefully, then smiled as he slightly crinkled his forehead. "I'm very sorry," he said in a soft, but resonating voice. "There's been some mistake here. Your card is unsigned. You will have to return at some later time."

As he returned the card to Evelyn, she received a strong telepathic impression from him that there would not be a death in her immediate family for another five years.

The last thing she remembered about her encounter with St. Peter at the gates of Heaven was the sight of her spirit family waving farewell to her as she started back down the white staircase.

"When I regained consciousness, I could hardly speak. The first thing that I managed to say to my mother, who was at the bedside, was, 'I couldn't get in because my card wasn't signed.' My husband and my brother were also in the room, and they started to laugh. There were tears in my husband's eyes as he gently embraced me, but he still had to tease me: 'Seven weeks we wait for a word from her, and what do we get? "I couldn't get in because my card wasn't signed!" ' "

Evelyn Lovell is convinced that she met St. Peter during her near-death experience. She knows that she might not be able to prove her contention to the skeptic, but she has the faith of her own conviction that it was so.

She does not know exactly when her near-death experience took place, for she suffered a severe concussion from the accident and she underwent five serious operations during the seven weeks that she was unconscious.

"My near-death experience could have occurred while I was lying in the driveway or sometime during my stay in the hospital. I don't really know. All I *do* know is that it really happened.

"While some people poked fun at me when I told them about my near-death experience and my meeting with St. Peter and all my deceased relatives, my mother and my grandmother believed me. I don't really need anyone to believe me, since I *know* what took place, but it is nice to have the support of Mom and Nana Jennings."

Certain researchers have developed the theory that we will all find what we expect to find on the other side. This hypothesis is based on the "thoughts are things" principle, which would be operative once the individual soul is freed from the limitations of a physical body. In essence, this theory suggests that the individual creates the afterlife he finds, either from faith or from the teachings that he or she received as a child.

Therefore, as a Christian, it is logical that Evelyn Lovell should find herself at the "gates of Heaven" with St. Peter appropriately overseeing his traditional role as the overseer of a new soul's right of entry.

In any case, whether allegory or other-dimensional reality, Evelyn Lovell's near-death experience was valid to her and provided a valuable aid in assisting a badly injured woman to more easily understand her personal journey from life ... to death ... and back again.

And by the way, St. Peter's prediction to Evelyn Lovell that there would not be a death in her immediate family for five years proved to be uncannily accurate. It was not until September of 1992, five years after her near-death experience, that her twenty-four-year-old niece was killed in an automobile accident.

• 18 •

He Was Ready to Cross the Threshold to Death

John Lowe was twenty-two years old when he miraculously lost his fear of death.

It was 1942. Lowe was a trooper with the Seventh Hussars, driving a light tank on the long retreat of the British forces in Burma. One March day while engaged in this action, he and two other troopers were traveling down a jungle road near Rangoon, fully aware that they were being hotly pursued by Japanese patrols.

Lowe and his buddies expected to be hit at any moment, because the jungle around them was filled with enemy soldiers.

"We turned on a curve in the road and saw two trees lying across the road. It was obvious that the Japanese had placed them there as a roadblock.

"The instant that we saw the block, we were on full alert, but it was already too late," Lowe said. "We scarcely had a chance to react when our light tank rolled over a land mine and was shattered."

Lowe's mates were killed instantly. Lowe was wounded, his shoulders sliced by shrapnel, but he managed to get out of the tank.

"As I tumbled down the side of the tank, I saw two Japanese soldiers, their rifles ready, coming slowly out of the jungle. We had run right into an ambush."

It was at that precise moment that John Lowe felt his Real Self slipping out of his body. With surprise, he saw that he was floating upward, high above the road.

Down below he could clearly see his bleeding body—and the two Japanese soldiers approaching it.

"Although it did not seem at all strange to me at the time," Lowe recalled, "I experienced a peculiar lack of interest in what might happen to my body.

"I could feel no pain, and I did not feel any particular remorse as I watched what I was certain would be my moment of death. It was very apparent that at any moment the two Japanese troops would either put a bullet in my back or ram a couple of bayonets into my chest.

"It was like being in a theater balcony looking down on the stage. I simply hovered above my injured physical body, awaiting the inevitable."

But before the Japanese soldiers could fire the fatal shot or administer the mortal bayonet thrust, a British tank that had been following Lowe's ambushed vehicle came "crashing down along the jungle track."

When the Japanese saw the metal monster bearing down on them, they immediately ran back into the underbrush for cover, forgetting all about delivering the death blow to the wounded Brit.

Lowe, still above it all in his aerial position, watched the British tank halt alongside the mine-blasted light tank. Two troopers, rifles in hand, advanced cautiously toward his body. It was a favorite Japanese trick to booby trap the bodies of the British troopers' fallen comrades.

The two soldiers quickly ascertained that although the other two crewmen of the light tank were dead, Lowe was still alive—and booby-trap free. The troopers gathered up the unconscious man's body and carried it back to their tank.

"They slipped my body in through the turret, and at that moment I must have returned to my physical body, because I felt pain for the first time—and immediately passed out again!

"The next thing that I remember," Lowe said,

"is waking up in the hospital, with bandages on my wounds."

Later that same day, when they learned that Lowe was fully conscious, the two troopers who had saved his life stopped by the field hospital to check on his progress.

"The instant the two blokes stepped through the hospital tent's flap I recognized them as the troopers who had lifted my body into the tank," Lowe said.

"They seemed astonished that I should know who they were, for they believed me to be unconscious all the time that they had carried me back to the hospital.

"I tried my best to explain to them that while my body truly had been totally unconscious, some other part of me—the Real Me—had been hovering somewhere above the bloody scene, calmly watching everything that was going on.

"I firmly believe that I was preparing for the end," Lowe said. "I am convinced that I was on the threshold of death and that my spirit was waiting to move on when the other tank crew came along that jungle road and saved my life."

Britain's Ministry of Defense, which keeps records of all of its armed forces, confirmed that Lowe had been seriously wounded in the explosion near Rangoon. He recovered from his wounds, however, and was able to serve throughout the remainder of the war.

Lowe, who was fifty when he made this report

in 1969, worked at that time in a factory in Tunstall, England.

"Despite being in the middle of death all of the time throughout the war, I never had any fear after that of death—and I still don't.

"I know that death is a place where pain and fear disappear, as it did for me over that jungle road."

Among the findings of a 1988 *Better Homes and Gardens* survey of 80,000 readers,

89 percent of the respondents said that they believed in eternal life;

87 percent envisioned a heaven;

86 percent believed in miracles.

Father Andrew Greeley, professor of sociology at the University of Arizona, together with colleagues at the University of Chicago, released such data as the following in the 1987 issue of *American Health*:

73 percent of the adult population in the United States believe in life after death;

68 percent perceive that afterlife to be Paradise;

and 74 percent expect to be reunited with their loved ones after death.

• 19 •

A Near-Fatal Accident and a Session with Her Guardian Angel Put Her Back on the Spiritual Path to the Light

On the night of November 20, 1983, Ingrid Dorstewitz of Duluth, Minnesota, went to bed in an very uncomfortable state of mental confusion. Her personal affairs and relationships had reached a critical stage, and she was badly in need of advice.

"I was twenty-eight years old, and I had always been fiercely independent," she said in her report of her experience. "But now I could see that what I had wished to term prideful self-reliance had in too many cases been nothing but stubborn bullheadedness. I was born under the sun sign of Taurus. Maybe it was beginning to show a bit too much."

Tossing fitfully throughout the night, Ingrid

rose before her alarm sounded and tried to jolt herself into wakefulness with strong, black coffee and an ice-cold shower.

She was so preoccupied with her problems and stresses that she backed her vintage Mustang directly into the path of an oncoming truck.

"Although it is sinful to admit even now," Ingrid confessed, "but a part of me was almost relieved when the truck compacted my little car and tossed it aside like a crushed tin can. I saw no way that I could get out of the crash alive—and when I found myself floating above the entire scene—and then soaring through what seemed like outer space, I made the logical assumption that I was dead."

The strange thing was that Ingrid did not perceive a brilliant light, a dark tunnel, or angelic guides, as have so many individuals who have undergone near-death experiences.

"I found myself at the entrance of a spacious park but everything was unnaturally silent. I mean, there should have been people streaming around; there should have been laughter, music, happy shouts. But the place seemed absolutely deserted."

Cautiously, Ingrid stood in her spirit body outside the large iron gates to the park. If they were, truly, the Gates to Heaven, she wasn't terribly certain that she wanted to be in a hurry to walk through. If this was a heavenly sphere, it was an awfully quiet and lonely one.

As she stood quietly evaluating the situation, a man dressed in the uniform and cap of a park keeper approached the gates from the inside.

They stared at each other for several moments before he asked her: "You coming in—or staying out?"

Ingrid shrugged. "It seems lonely in there. Aren't there any others?"

The park keeper shook his head. "Not right now. Sometimes it's best to be alone."

"But . . . but . . . alone up here?" Ingrid wondered.

"You coming in—or staying out?"

"I can't decide."

"Do you always need help making decisions?" The park keeper seemed a bit exasperated. "The biggest decisions we ever make, we have to make alone."

Before Ingrid could say another word, she was astonished to see the park keeper begin to change before her eyes.

"Instead of the park uniform, he now wore a glittering, silklike tunic that came to his knees. Around his middle was a belt of silver. His arms and legs were bare, but they seemed to be glowing and giving forth a light of purity and holiness. His face was brightest of all."

The light being beckoned for Ingrid to come nearer to him, but she was momentarily in awe of his majestic appearance.

But after a moment or two of careful scrutiny,

she suddenly exclaimed: "I know you! I used to see you all the time when I was a little girl. You're my guardian angel."

The angelic entity smiled and nodded agreement. "For a while there, I didn't think you would remember me."

"Well," Ingrid protested defensively, "as a park keeper?"

"No! As you saw me as a child," he quickly chided her. "You shut your ears to me and my guidance a long time ago."

Ingrid lowered her eyes, feeling suddenly very uncomfortable.

"Ah, child, when you reached those teenage years! You wanted no counsel other than your own. You turned your back on your parents, your pastor—and certainly on me, the still, small voice inside your head. You suddenly thought that you already knew it all—and what you didn't know, you seemed to think that you would invent."

"I was exercising my free will," Ingrid offered in a feeble attempt at defense.

Her guardian angel snorted. "Free will! Liberty of spirit, my child, is not license of the flesh."

Ingrid looked around her. They were still all alone. "So this is the place where you list all my sins. We're going to be here for quite a while."

The angel shook his head. "I've been through a lot with you, but thankfully the itemization of sins, misdeeds, and lack of good judgment is not in my department.

"What so many of you humans never seem to realize is that we angels are not tattletales or spies or intercessors to take your bruises and bumps on our own ethereal bodies. It is so plainly written in all the holy books that humans and angels are to work together in the service of one God.

"I have thought long and hard about why humans find this so hard to be true, and I have concluded that it is because they give too much thought to the material things of Earth and too little thought to the everlasting virtues and truths.

"And, my little Ingrid, isn't that the largest share of your problems right now? You've become an opportunist who will achieve success no matter what it takes, no matter who you have to step on. You've resorted to lying, cheating, seducing, deceiving. I can't believe that this is what has become of my sweet little Ingrid, who used to be so devout and mindful of the feelings of others."

Ingrid frowned. "It's tough down there. Besides, where were you when I really needed you?"

"Everything that has happened to you has been part of the testing program of Earth," he told her. "In a very real sense, it is a kind of schoolhouse down there. You have to pass certain tests before you can advance to the next grade."

"Well"—Ingrid nodded toward the iron gates—"I guess it's too late for me to try to pass any more tests. Looks like I flunked."

"You need have no fear, child. There are no tortures or punishments that await you here. Love is the guiding principle of this sphere. The judgment that you dread has already begun. Already you lie awake nights punishing yourself. You have already begun to mete out punishment to yourself.

"You made reference to free will earlier. In recent weeks, you have been punishing yourself of your own free will by reviewing the life that you have led. And as you bravely own up to one sin after another, you will begin once again to progress on the spiritual path. You have already inflicted a great deal of punishment on yourself during the dark nights of the soul that you have recently endured.

"You will return to the physical body that you inhabit on Earth, because, I am grateful to report, you have been assessed as one for whom enlightenment is still possible. You have already been undergoing a process of evaluating the false idols of earth plane existence and finding them very lacking in lasting worth.

"Frequently, we are obliged to call the spirits of such stubborn ones as yourself away from the earth plane so that we might refresh your vision of your true spiritual mission on your life path."

It was at this point in her near-death, out-of-body experience that Ingrid was shown a vision by her guardian angel that she can only describe was "completely ineffable . . . beyond all words and the power of human speech."

She only has been able to preserve a very fleeting image of soaring through a star-decked universe in which every atom of matter seemed intelligent and throbbing with Divine Love.

"And then," she said, "I seemed to be moving toward the center of all creation, toward God, toward a brilliant light. And then I became One with the Light. Totally, completely, One with the Light."

When she regained consciousness in the hospital, Ingrid was told that she had been in a coma for four days. During visiting hours, she was astonished to see standing behind her mother the suitor whom she had recently rejected with harsh and unkind words.

"I thought you might like to have a friend," he said hesitatingly. "I mean, you know, to get some things for you and stuff."

Ingrid stretched forth her hand and gripped his forearm. "I *need* you and I need your love," she told him with sincerity and humility. "Can you forgive my cruel tongue and bad manners?"

"I already have," he told her with a warm smile.

After she was released from the hospital, Ingrid said that she worked very hard and diligently at straightening out her business, as well as her personal relationships. Although these tasks were very time-consuming, she admitted, she stressed the point that she would never allow them to cause her to stray once again from the true purpose for her life on Earth—to grow in spiritual light and to work always for the Oneness.

· 20 ·

He Saw His Physical Body Like an "Old Coat" to Be Discarded

In the December 1952, issue of *Fate* magazine, Paul M. Vest tells of the time that he was swimming in the ocean and found to his awful fear that the current was too strong for him.

He became alarmed, shouting for help, but the wind was blowing against him, and he was really too far out for his voice to have carried to shore under the best of conditions.

He fought with all his strength to best the powerful undertow—but then a large wave pounded him under the water.

In the next instant, Vest was no longer in his drowning body.

"As swift as a flash my consciousness—or self—had withdrawn to a distance ten or twelve feet above and was looking down at my body floundering in the sea," he said.

Vest's body had not entirely lost consciousness. It flailed its arms spasmodically and kicked and fought for breath.

His "I" consciousness remained above, serene, calm, almost disinterested in the fate of the physical body. The "I" consciousness knew ". . . with absolute certainty that [it] was timeless, ageless, and eternal. Thus it watched the drowning body dispassionately as you might watch an old coat being discarded."

With the same disinterest, the "I" consciousness observed swimmers arriving to rescue the physical body and to bring it unconscious to shore.

Only when the body began to respond to artificial respiration did the "I" begin to be drawn back to the physical shell by an "irresistible force." The essential self of Paul M. Vest seemed almost reluctant to have to put on the cumbersome apparatus of a physical body once again.

"Since that day," Vest wrote, "I no longer think of my body as 'I' any more than I would think of one of my garments as 'I.' "

· 21 ·

A Near-Death Experience After a Vicious Assault Brings the Victim to the Arms of Jesus

A young woman who prefers to be known only as Carol for purposes of anonymity told me of a near-death experience which occurred to her after she had been sexually assaulted and beaten.

"One of the strangest things about that whole experience is that all day long I had had an uneasy feeling that something bad was going to happen to me," Carol said. "I was nervous all day, perhaps especially at work. I think I remember that it was also the full moon."

At that time, Carol explained, she considered herself a totally practical, realistic person. She didn't believe in omens or anything mystical. She swears that she didn't even believe in woman's intuition.

But later that night, as she lay on her bed, she felt the need to pray.

"At that point in my life, I only related to Jesus as an abstract entity, but it felt reassuring somehow to be praying to something outside of myself," Carol said.

It was while she was lying on her bed, praying, that the attack occurred.

"He was just there, as if he had appeared from the darkness in a corner of my bedroom. Later, the police said that he had got in through a window near the fire escape, because they found where he had bent the bars. They theorized that he had hidden in my room, maybe waiting for hours for me to come home.

"He was my worst nightmare come to life. He started punching me in the face even before he started ripping at my nightgown. I remember trying to say something, begging him to stop, and then he must have hit me with a club or something."

Carol was found by her landlady the next morning. It was a three full days before she regained consciousness.

"My spirit or soul, the Real Me, left my body right after my attacker struck me with that heavy blunt object. It seemed as though I was traveling faster than the speed of light, literally hurling through the cosmos.

"I don't know how many light-years I was away from Earth when I saw the most beautiful light imaginable. I felt myself drifting toward it—and then for a few brief moments of divine love and ecstasy, I became unified with it.

"This intensely glorified state may have lasted for seconds or for hours or for days."

Carol paused in the telling of her story. "This part always sounds like I'm some kind of egomaniac or something," she apologized. "I'm not saying that I saw Jesus to make myself sound special or important or holy. It was just an experience that happened to me."

I encouraged Carol to tell her account simply and directly. I told her that I would not judge her or her experience on any kind of scale of correctness or propriety and that she should grant herself the same nonjudgmental attitude.

She smiled and continued her account:

"I had been praying to Jesus for guidance just before the attack took place," she reminded me, "now, somewhere out there in space or Heaven or wherever, I saw an image of Jesus on the cross.

"And then I saw an image of *myself* on the cross, and I realized that my physical body was undergoing a kind of crucifixion.

"That terrible image of myself on the cross only lasted for a few seconds, and then I more or less felt myself being filled with what I can only call the 'Eve consciousness.' I felt as though

I was Everywoman, and I felt the sorrow of my sisters throughout all of time. I felt the pain of all those women who had been assaulted, raped, and victimized by beings of negative consciousness.

"And then it was as if Jesus himself was inviting me to sit beside him beneath an olive tree in this beautiful garden. I say it was Jesus, because the being was so filled with light that it hurt even my spirit eyes to look directly at him for very long at a time."

The illuminated being that Carol was convinced was Jesus, put his arm around her in a brotherly fashion and comforted her for the torment which her body was presently enduring.

"He told me that my spirit had been about to receive an illumination experience, that my physical and spiritual vibrations had been about to be raised. Often when this is about to occur, a negative being will be attracted to the positive vibrations. The man who had attacked me had been possessed by such a negative being."

Carol expressed wonder that she had been singled out to be blessed by such a high-energy spiritual experience as illumination. "I told Jesus that I wasn't a very good churchgoer, and that I really hadn't lived anything near a saintly life."

According to Carol, Jesus told her that she had always been one of his special children, even though she had strayed from his flock from time to time. The angels had been about to visit her to begin to prepare her for a change in life-style.

"It was written in the Divine Plan that you would soon be leaving your present work and begin to work with youthful runaways and the homeless," Jesus told her. "If only you had permitted yourself to become more attuned to the ministry of Light on Earth, you would have been better prepared for the possibility of attack by a negative entity."

When Carol wondered why her angels hadn't intervened and protected her, Jesus answered that Satan was the Lord of the Earth and exerted much power in the lower kingdoms.

"Your angels can only inspire you to act and offer instructions on how you may protect yourself," he said. "That was why you were led to pray, my child. If only you had sought the assistance of the higher-plane beings sooner, your angels would have found some way to advise you how to protect yourself. Remember, the Scripture always admonishes you to 'ask and you shall receive.' But those of you on Earth must always be the ones who do the knocking at the door to Heaven. Angels cannot interfere with the lessons that you choose to learn on Earth."

Carol could not avoid asking *the* question any longer. "Am I dead? Is that why I am here? Is that why I am talking to you? Am I in Heaven?"

The illuminated being shook his head and laughed. "No, my child, you are not dead. Soon your angels will return you to your physical body and you will be able to resume your destiny."

Carol expressed outrage over the physical assault that had just taken place upon her material self.

"As foul and base as such acts by negative entities may be, my child, you will rise above such abuse of the physical self and conduct your mission on Earth without anger or bitterness."

Carol wondered if she had the strength to do so.

Jesus told her that now she would walk only in Divine Love. "You will be an apostle of Divine Love and you will teach many others by your example.

"Divine Love is the one great power that moves the universe. Divine Love is the force that makes men and women think and do those things that create peace and goodwill.

"On Earth," the illuminated being continued, "very few humans possess the full power of Divine Love—yet the influence of those few is felt all over the planet.

"Even those who have never heard of my teachings or those of my Father, enjoy the benefit of Divine Love in some kind of belief or faith in an overshadowing spirit of great power and watchfulness. So even though my gospel may not be preached to every corner of Earth, the

Love of the Divine is everywhere and is all-pervading.

"It is only Divine Love that can alter the material and the animal in humans and awaken within them their godlike potential. It is only Divine Love that can transform the human into the angelic.

"But please understand," Jesus qualified for Carol, "even though a man or a woman can be filled with Divine Love to the highest degree, such energy will still not make them a god-being or equal to the Father in any of his powers and attributes. This cannot be. But the infusion of Divine Love will make all those who possess it like the Father in love, harmony, happiness, and good works.

"Divine Love has no counterpart in all creation. It changes not; it cannot be corrupted, and it has the power to transform the most hardened sinner into a true child of God.

"Go now, Carol," Jesus bade her. "Return to your world as an emissary of Divine Love."

When she awakened in the hospital, her mother was at her bedside. Carol accepted her mother's embrace and her tears with deep appreciation, but then she informed her that she was all right, that she had been reborn in the arms of Jesus. There was nothing that anyone could ever do to her physical body that could touch her soul, enveloped as it was in Divine Love.

As soon as she had recovered from the traumatic effects of the brutal assault, Carol resigned from her job and took a position with social services in a major city in California. For the last ten years she has worked extensively with runaway children and given freely of her time to establishing homes and jobs for the elderly and the homeless.

· 22 ·

The Extraordinary Near-Death Experiences of Two Medical Doctors

When the Royal Medical Society of Edinburgh met on February 26, 1937, Sir Auckland Geddes, a medical doctor and professor of anatomy, read a most unusual paper before the august body of medical professionals.

A colleague who had requested anonymity had recorded a near-death experience which he wished to bring to the attention of his fellow members of the healing profession.

According to this anonymous physician, he had been near death and had at the same time been conscious of being outside his body. Upon his recovery, he had immediately undertaken to dictate his amazing experience to his secretary.

One evening, shortly after midnight, the doctor was stricken with acute gastroenteritis, so severe that by ten o'clock the following morning he was too ill even to ring for assistance. However, though the doctor's body was in terrible agony, his mental processes remained quite clear, and he began to review his financial affairs, firmly convinced that his death was imminent.

While thus engaged, he suddenly realized ". . . my consciousness was separating from another consciousness, which was also 'me.' " Later, while dictating, he labeled these two states of consciousness "A" and "B." His ego—or spiritual essence—aligned itself with the "A" state of consciousness. The "B" consciousness remained with the physical body.

The physician observed that as his physical health deteriorated further the "B" personality began to fade, while the "A" personality began more and more to embody his complete self. As the process continued, the "A" personality vacated the physical body entirely, and he was able to observe his body lying inert in bed.

As his awareness of the situation increased, he realized that not only could he see his physical body, but he could also perceive his entire house and his garden in London. Testing his new range of beingness, he soon discovered that he could instantly travel to Scotland or to any other place that occurred to him.

At about this time he became aware of the presence of a guide or "mentor," who explained to him that he was ". . . free in a time dimension of space, wherein *now* was equivalent to *here* in the ordinary three-dimensional space of everyday life."

With the new understanding related to him by his guide, the doctor next noted that he was able to see things in four or more dimensional places. At the same time, he could see equally well in the three-dimensional space of everyday life.

In his report to the medical society, the physician apologized for his lack of words to describe his extraordinary experience. No words seemed adequate to put forth his actual feelings and sensations.

His mentor, he said, impressed on him that ". . . all our brains are just end-organs projecting as it were from the three-dimensional universe into the psychic stream . . . and flowing with it into the fourth and the fifth dimensions."

Accordingly, the doctor commented, he could see this "condensation of the psychic stream" forming a kind of cloud around each living brain.

His guide further explained that the fourth dimension existed, correspondingly, in everything that existed in the three-dimensional space. Moreover, everything in the third dimension also existed in the fourth and fifth.

"*Now* in the fourth-dimensional universe is equal to *here* in the three-dimensional universe. A fourth-dimensional being is *everywhere* in the now . . . just as one is *everywhere* in the *here* in a three-dimensional view of things."

In the present state of his existence, the doctor's guide pointed out that he was a blue-colored cloud.

Many more mysteries were being revealed to the physician when one of his servants entered the bedroom and discovered with horror his dying body.

He watched his servant rush to the telephone and place a hasty call to a doctor who was a colleague. At the same time, he could see that physician take leave of his patients because of the frantic emergency.

When his colleague arrived, the doctor's "A" consciousness could hear the man think: "He is nearly gone!"

He was able to hear the man speaking to him, but he was unable to respond. He was no longer in the "B" consciousness that resided in his physical body.

The visiting doctor pulled a syringe out of his medical bag. The "A" consciousness of the physician saw this act and became very angry. It did not wish to return to the "B" consciousness.

As the injection flowed into the doctor's body, however, the "A" consciousness once again began to take notice of his heartbeat and gradually allowed itself to be pulled back into the physical body. Finally, the doctor became fully aware of himself once again and discovered himself lying in disarray on his bed.

"I was intensely annoyed," the anonymous doctor related in his narrative, "because I had become so interested in the process and I was just beginning to understand where I was and what I was seeing.

"I came back into my body, really angry at being pulled back; and once back, all the clarity of the vision of everything disappeared, and I was again possessed of a glimmer of consciousness which was suffused with pain."

Reiterating his firm belief that his near-death experience had shown no tendency to ". . . fade like a dream would fade . . . nor to grow . . . or to rationalize itself," he stressed his contention that the experience held momentous import not only for himself, but for every human being.

Sir Auckland Geddes completed the reading of his anonymous colleague's near-death experience and confronted the members of the society with his own concluding remarks:

"Of one thing we can be quite sure—it was not fake. Without that certainty I should not have brought it to your notice. My colleague's experience has helped me to define the idea of a psychic continuum in which we all exist.

"Furthermore, he has brought telepathy, clairvoyance . . . indeed, all of the parapsychic manifestations into the domain of the picturable."

When Dr. Wiltse of Skiddy, Kansas, felt that he was dying, he called to his family and friends and bade them farewell.

His attending physician, Dr. Raynes, later testified to the Society for Psychical Research (Volume VII of the *Proceedings*) that for the duration of four hours, Dr. Wiltse lay without pulse or perceptible heartbeat. Dr. Raynes did state, however, that he may have perceived an occasional, very slight gasp from his patient.

During this lengthy period of clinical death, Dr. Wiltse found himself in what he later termed a state of "conscious existence" that bore no relationship to his physical body.

Immersed in this new state of consciousness, the inquisitive Dr. Wiltse decided to try a few experiments.

He began to rock back and forth, trying to break the tenuous bond of tissues and fibers within his physical form. At length, he said, he began ". . . to feel and to hear the snappings of innumerable small cords," and he began to retreat from his feet toward his head as "a rubber cord shortens."

Shortly after that, the doctor felt his true self to be somehow gathered in the area of his head, where he emerged through the sutures of the skull.

"I recollect distinctly," he told the society in his report, "how I appeared to myself something like a jellyfish as regards to color and form."

As his true self emerged from his skull, Dr. Wiltse experienced the floating sensation so common to near-death projections. He felt himself bobbing gently up and down until his exertions landed him squarely on the floor.

At that point, he gradually arose and expanded himself to the full stature of his regular physical body.

"I seemed to be translucent, of a bluish cast, and perfectly naked," he said.

The doctor cast a glance at his woeful physical body on the sickbed, and he decided that he had no further use for it. Without further ado, he headed for the front door.

As he reached the door, Dr. Wiltse observed that he was suddenly fully clothed. At the same time, he noted that two of his friends were standing by the door and that they were completely unaware of his presence.

With a great deal of surprise and amusement, Dr. Wiltse discovered that he could pass directly through his friends and continue on out through the door.

"I never saw the street more distinctly than I saw it then," he stated. "Glancing around, I noticed that I was attached by means of a small cord, like a spider's web, to my body in the house."

Then all at once the doctor found himself soaring high above the neighborhood, quite enjoying the aerial view that his unique situation afforded him.

Just as he was relaxing into his newly achieved emancipation from the confines of bodily flesh, however, Dr. Wiltse found himself on a road with steep rocks blocking his journey.

He attempted to climb around them; but as he was doing so, a black cloud surrounded him—and he found himself back in his bedroom, once more confined to an ill body.

Perhaps certain readers are mentally bringing up a rather mundane but interesting point at this time: Why is it that those who undergo near-death experiences usually see themselves clothed—when they are amorphous substances—rather than naked, as Dr. Wiltse at first perceived his body?

It is my personal theory that since near-death experiences involve the essential stuff of human personality, the soul body, the projected mind may—if it wishes to do so—"create" its clothing by exercising the same kind of mental machinery that is utilized in dreams.

I think the case of Dr. Wiltse provides us with a very good look at some of the mechanics of the near-death experience.

When he first projects from the skull, he perceives himself as "something like a jellyfish as regards color and form." Then, because his mind—what the anonymous doctor termed the

"B" consciousness—had been conditioned on the temporal plane to think in terms of physical body concepts, the "jellyfish" expands into the full stature of a naked human male.

A few moments later when Dr. Wiltse confronts his sober-faced friends at the door, he suddenly finds himself clothed. Even though he is certain that they cannot see him in his spiritual body, a lifetime on the Earth plane and in a particular culture had conditioned him not to conceive of himself going about in the nude.

As we have seen in other case histories in this book, many men and women who have projected free of the Earth plane in their near-death experiences are more likely to discard temporal plane concepts of "body" and "clothing" and often report perceiving themselves as a "shiny cloud," a "bright balloon," an "egg yolk," or "something like a jellyfish." Although Dr. Wiltse's case is very dramatic, it would appear that he remained pretty much bound to the lower physical planes of reality until he was revived on his sickbed.

It is also worth noting in the Dr. Wiltse case that his near-death experience terminated when he was confronted by steep rocks that blocked his journey.

Generally speaking, there seem to be two types of environment for near-death experiences:

1. The environment of this planet Earth, in which the projected personality observes the ac-

tions of people in faraway places and sees actual occurrences at great distances which can later be substantiated.

2. The environment of other planes of existence or dimensions of reality in which the projected personality may encounter entities which he perceives as angels, masters, guides, saints, or the spirits of loved ones who have previously passed away. The geography of these spiritual planes seems to be quite similar to that of Earth and depending upon the religious views of the projector is often interpreted as Heaven, Paradise, or a place of eternal bliss.

The "rocks" that halted Dr. Wiltse's advance may indeed have been rocks on another plane of existence—or they may have been formed by his own mental machinery as a symbol that he was not to venture farther, but was to return to his physical body.

H. H. Price, a former president of the British Society for Psychical Research, has put forth the view that the whole point of our life on Earth might very well be to provide us with a stockpile of memories out of which we might construct a meaningful image-world at the time of our death. Such a world would be a psychological world and not a physical one, even though it seems to be quite physical to those who would experience it.

In Volume 5, Number 1 of *Tomorrow*, Price conjectures that the other world ". . . would be the manifestation in image form of the memories and desires of its inhabitants, including their repressed or unconscious memories and desires. It might be every bit as detailed, as vivid, and complex as this present perceptible world which we experience now.

"We may note that it might well contain a vivid and persistent image of one's own body.

"The surviving personality, according to this concept of survival, is in actual fact an immaterial entity. But if one habitually *thinks* of oneself as embodied (as one well might, at least for a considerable time), an image of one's own body might be, as it were, the persistent center of one's image world, much as the perceived physical body is the persistent center of one's perceptible world in this present life."

· 23 ·

Researching New Proofs of Life After Death

During a terrible accident in 1982, Massachusetts State Trooper Lorraine Roy, thirty-seven, was smashed against a concrete road barrier by an automobile. She suffered massive internal injuries.

Officer Roy was given the last rites by a hospital chaplain; for at one point, according to her attending physician, she was clinically dead.

"I think perhaps I did die, but my dead father met me and sent me back," Lorraine said.

"I remember thinking that I wasn't going to make it. Then I became aware that my father, who died five years earlier, was there at the end of a tunnel. It was a warm, loving feeling.

"I had the sense that I was dying. 'Maybe I'll be joining you, Daddy,' I said to him.

"He smiled at me and called me by my nickname. 'Not yet, Lolo, not yet,' he said gently. 'You're going to be all right. Go back now. It's not your time.' "

In the 1960s, Dr. Eugene E. Bernard, professor of psychology at North Carolina State University, conducted an extensive study of out-of-body experience [OBE] and suggested that one out of every one hundred persons has experienced out-of-body projection.

The psychologist found out that OBE most often occurs during time of stress, during natural childbirth, during minor surgery, at times of extreme fear, and, of course, during instances of near-death.

In his *Life at Death*, published in 1980, Kenneth Ring released the results of data that he had compiled from 102 men and women who had provided him with their NDE accounts. In his assessment of their reports, Ring tabulated that 60 percent of the subjects found that the near-death experience had brought them a sense of peace; 37 percent reported a separation of consciousness from the physical body; 23 percent mentioned the process of entering a dark tunnel; 16 percent said that they had seen the light;

and 10 percent claimed that they had entered the light.

A survey conducted in 1991 by Dr. Colin Ross, associate professor of psychiatry at the University of Manitoba in Winnipeg, suggests that as many as one in three people have left their bodies and returned—most often during times of crisis, extreme pain, and near-death.

A recent Gallup Poll revealed that 15 percent of all Americans claim to have had a near-death experience.

Dr. Bruce Greyson, professor of psychiatry at the University of Connecticut Health Center, says that his studies indicate that as many as eight million Americans have undergone a near-death-experience that completely transformed their lives.

A Macho Marine Is Transformed After a Near-Death-Experience

When he went overseas to do his hitch in Vietnam, Steve Price was a gung-ho Marine.

A few months later, seriously wounded in action, he suddenly found himself surrounded by a brilliant white light that seemed to embrace him and bathe him in the most peaceful, joyous feeling imaginable. Soon, he found himself in a beautiful garden, but an angel waved him back, telling him that it was not yet his time.

And then he was in his hospital room, still filled with peace, as if he had been born anew.

Today Price is a laboratory technician, who describes himself as "mild-mannered, thoughtful, and a lot different from the hard-charging macho marine I used to be."

Two Angels Brought Her Back to Her Children

In 1988, Susan Gallagher, thirty-one, a mother of three children, died during surgery and found herself floating in the spirit world.

She was met by two angels, and she told them frankly that she could not join them at that time. Her children still needed her.

The angels nodded in silent agreement, and Susan floated back to her body.

Feeling God's Presence Converted a Hard-nosed Cop to an Educator

Joe Geraci was a no-nonsense, hard-nosed cop for ten years before his heart stopped beating during surgery.

While the doctors worked desperately to save his life, Geraci felt the presence of God in Paradise. He left the hospital a changed man, quit the police force, and became a district coordinator for the public school system.

Becoming One with the Light Changes Materialistic Student to Social Worker

In 1970, Kimberly Clark Sharp collapsed and was rushed to a hospital. Emergency medical workers accidentally hooked a ventilator incorrectly and sucked all the air out of her lungs instead of pumping oxygen into her.

Kimberly became engulfed in a blinding white light that answered any question she mentally asked. She was ecstatic, but the Light told her that she must return to Earth to help others.

Kimberly returned to life and changed from a "shallow, materialistic, lazy" twenty-one-year-old college student to the social worker that she is today.

Two Dying Children Meet Loved Ones on the Other Side

In July of 1988, I told journalist Paul Bannister about two cases of life after death which involved young children which I had recently uncovered at that time.

In Chicago, a twelve-year-old girl died on the operating table, but she was later revived. Later, she told her parents, "I wasn't afraid. I was met by a very nice boy who said that he was my dead brother. He wrapped me in a wonderful feeling of love and caring. It was so lovely, but who could it have been? I don't have a dead brother."

The parents broke down and wept. Their daughter did not know it, but she had had a brother who had died when she would have been too young to remember him. The parents had never told her about him because the loss had been so painful.

In another case from the Chicago area, I was informed of a case in which a young girl, dying of cancer, told her parents in the last minutes before she passed away, "I have to go now. Grandmother is waiting for me. And look! There's Joanie. What's she doing here? Joanie isn't dead."

The child died then, calmly and quietly, leaving her parents in shock—because they knew, but had not told their daughter, that her best friend, Joanie, had been killed two weeks earlier in an auto accident.

Near-Death Experiences Can Enhance Talents and Abilities

Bannister also interviewed my longtime friend and fellow researcher, Phyllis Atwater of Charlottesville, Virginia, who nearly died after hemmorrhaging in 1977. After her own dramatic experience, Phyllis began to investigate other cases of NDE in which ordinary men and women had survived near-death.

Today, she has written a number of books on the subject (such as *Coming Back to Life*) and has instructed many people how to develop their own psychic sensitivity. In 1988, she explained that she had ". . . interviewed more than two hundred NDE survivors and found that their experiences had triggered something in them so that certain abilities were enhanced."

Phyllis provided a remarkable illustration in the case of a truck driver who survived a near-fatal crash and who subsequently began to display advanced mathematical abilities:

"Overnight, he was showing gifted abilities in higher physics. He was able to write down complicated mathematical equations he had no clue about—and they were correct. Gradually, he came to understand them, and he still has his new abilities today."

The Near-Death Experience May Bring About an Acceleration of ESP

Dr. Melvin Morse, clinical associate professor of pediatrics at the University of Washington, is another NDE researcher who has found that certain survivors of the near-death experience return with enhanced abilities. Dr. Morse, author of *Transformed by the Light,* has noted that some of the people he interviewed came back to life with "an increase in the amount of electrical energy their bodies emit," an acceleration of intellect and/or psychic abilities, and even the power to heal themselves.

In one of his investigations, Dr. Morse spoke to a forty-five-year-old woman named Kathy who said that she had been afflicted with incurable thyroid cancer and had been given six months to live. It was at that awful point that she also developed pneumonia.

After she was rushed to a hospital, her heart stopped; and as doctors worked desperately to revive her, Kathy stated that the real her was "high on top of a beautiful ridge overlooking a beautiful valley. The colors were extremely vivid, and I was filled with joy."

A Light Being touched her spirit body, and her entire essence "was filled with its light."

Later, when she was revived, Kathy's pneumonia had disappeared. A few weeks later, her cancer, too, had inexplicably left her.

Dr. Morse told writer Don Gentile that he believed that Kathy's NDE had a direct influence on healing the cancer. He also stated that he had studied instances in which near-death survivors had returned to life a great deal more intelligent than they had been before the experience.

He Brought Back an Ancient Japanese Art from the Other World

Journalist Silvio Piersanti has investigated the case of Ligustro Berio, an installer of olive presses, who suffered a heart attack in 1972 and lapsed into a coma. When the resident of

Oneglia, Italy, recovered, he discovered that he suddenly had the talent to create valuable masterpieces in the style of ancient Japanese master painters.

Today, the now-seventy-year-old retired technician, who has never been to Japan and who has never had an art lesson in his life, spends up to two months to complete one of the remarkable prints, which sometimes include up to 180 colors.

Jack Hiller, who appraises Japanese art for Sotheby's in London, told Piersanti that Berio's ability was ". . . at the high level of top Japanese artists."

Japanese art critic Fukada Kazuhiko of Tokyo declared Berio's prints to be an ". . . incredible, unexplainable, yet perfect revival of an ancient Japanese technique."

Berio told Piersanti that life began for him after his experience with death. "Before my heart attack, I'd never even picked up a pencil to draw a picture."

• 24 •

He Returned with the Gift of Heavenly Music in His Fingertips

Sometimes it seems that the cosmic process of becoming one with the Light can stimulate any of the five senses or even activate talents and abilities that had previously lain unknown within the psyche of a person who survived a near-death experience.

In the mid-1970s, I investigated the case of an Iowa college student who returned from a blending with the Light and found that he had the ability to do many things which he had never before thought possible.

Martin, as I shall call him, had been reared in a strict Missouri Synod Lutheran farm family. Although he had always had a pleasant singing voice, he had never received any formal musical training and he had never taken a piano lesson in his life. Then, after becoming one with the Light, he found that he could sit down at the piano and play lovely melodies which just "came to him."

I sent a tape recording of Martin's celestial melodies to the president-elect of the National Association of Jazz Educators, who was also on the staff of the music department at a college in California. His analysis of the music which was being played by a young man who had never received even one elementary piano lesson was as follows:

"The left-hand accompaniment, for the most part, is a technique called an 'Alberti bass,' indicating a method of rhythmically playing the underlying harmony in such a manner that a continuous rhythmic flow is maintained, giving a forward motion to the accompaniment. This style of left-hand accompaniment did not come into common practice until the classical period, roughly 1750–1825.

"Although the left hand is in a classical-period style, the melodic and harmonic structure is modal, using the miolydian (sol, la, ti, do, re, mi, fa, sol), lydian (fa, sol, etc.) and dorian (re, mi, fa, etc.) modes. This modal and harmonic structure is not characteristic of the classical period, which was pretty much major-minor oriented in harmonic structure. The modal structure is very characteristic of current rock and folk tunes and/or the harmonizations used by sixteenth- and seventeenth-century solo singers (galliards, minstrels, etc.)."

In the opinion of my learned musicologist, Martin's celestial music reflected no particular well-known composer of any recent historical period. His music could somehow be the result of "extremely well-developed tonal memory and facile muscle-memory," and he could be "reproducing what he has heard and stored in his unconscious."

On the other hand, my expert was bold enough to speculate that the college student might be temporarily possessed when he entered the light, trancelike state which seemed always to precede his playing.

"Some soul wandering the astral world, who was a former musician-composer, possibly frustrated in his attempts at recognition, might be using this boy to get attention," he theorized.

He went on to add that reincarnation might also offer an explanation for an ostensible musical illiterate suddenly being able to compose music at the piano.

One night, while in the company of a clergyman and other professional and laymen and-

women, Martin went into trance and delivered a
message from a higher-plane spirit being or angelic entity, who claimed to originate from
". . . the light of the triad, the symbol of peace,
unity, understanding, and the achievement of
oneness."

The citizen of the heavenly realms, speaking
through Martin, advised those present to "reach
inside and bring forth the knowledge from
within. Become as one with the Light. Try to
work for all—not just for self alone."

When the angelic entity was asked if it had
come from a universal source or from an individ-
ualized consciousness, it replied:

"The source lies in no area, because it is the
area. It is of consciousness, yet it is of things that
are not seen, not heard of, not thought of. It
composes all, and yet it is one.

"Universal mind is a reference to a being,
yet to comprehend this, one must visualize an
Allness, a Oneness with the Light. This is the
Mind—the consciousness, the awareness of all
that there is and was and will be. The Mind is
all; you are all together to form the Oneness."

One of those present was concerned whether
or not an individual had to put away his or her
physical personality in order to become attuned
to the Oneness.

"The self draws from the central Source. You
are as one with it—yet the main difference is the
awareness and the degree that one is with it. To

put the self back in the central Source is to become as pure as One."

Of great interest to all those assembled that evening was the question of the principle of the continuation of life after physical death.

"As Oneness with the Light, we all have the same beginnings and the same ends.

"When one is born, he or she is in complete attunement with the God Mind; but the imperfections of the physical plane creates ego and its need to think of itself and no one else. Therefore, human beings must try to return to God Mind by using imperfect vehicles. Thus, it may take a series of times before they develop fully, before they evolve to become one with the God Mind.

"Human beings must experience all the pain and suffering that they have caused other beings which were created from the God Mind. This need to experience results in the cycle of lives dying and being reborn until the imperfections are alleviated or brought forth."

Another of the group wanted to know about the position of Jesus of Nazareth in the God Mind.

"Full comprehension of this entity cannot be contained in one physical mind, yet this is to be told: The entity called Yesu of Nazareth is of one attunement with the One Mind. Throughout his entire life, he maintained spiritual attunement with the Universal Mind. He had no death, because death only exists on a physical plane. His death was not spiritual, and the spirit is the true body. His body died because of the man-substance within it—yet his spirit lived and became alive again."

• 25 •

Three Famous Actors Describe Their Near-Death Experiences

It was about 1970, when he was filming a movie in Europe, that actor Donald Sutherland, star of such motion pictures as M*A*S*H, Invasion of the Body Snatchers, and Six Degrees of Separation, "died" and received a dramatic glimpse of life beyond the grave.

"I was out of my body—sort of floating to the ceiling," Sutherland told Ray Finch (Globe, February 27, 1990).

"Then I saw the 'blue tunnel' to eternity—it's what people often describe when they have after-death experiences."

Sutherland explained that his near-death experience occurred when he nearly succumbed to spinal meningitis.

"If I had stayed dead, I know I would have gone through the tunnel—and I am still intrigued by what I would have found.

"I can remember people discussing my death. They had sent a cable to my wife, telling her they would ship the body—meaning me—home.

"She flew to London and made all the funeral arrangements. Then she came to the hospital and discovered I was still alive."

In the autumn of 1989, while we were interviewing motion picture stars and searching out haunted sites in Hollywood for our book *Hollywood and the Supernatural*, my wife Sherry and I had the opportunity to interview actor Clint Walker, the star of the popular television Western series, *Cheyenne*, and such films as *The Dirty Dozen* and *The White Buffalo*. Walker, a big man who stands about six-feet-six, told us the fascinating story of his near-death experience which occurred during a skiing accident.

Walker had taken a serious spill going downhill which concluded with the sharp end of a ski pole being driven through his breastbone and piercing his heart.

"I became fascinated by what I saw coming out of my chest," Walker told us. "I saw 'rings' emanating from my wound. There was one ring after another. They looked just like smoke rings.

"I closed my eyes—and I was not just floating above my body . . . I was up above the world.

"I could see the planet getting smaller and smaller, and it came to me that our world was just a dirty, little old bus stop in the universe.

"I saw, too, that time was an illusion. I could see the true nature of things so much more clearly. I realized that I had always seen 'through a glass darkly,' and for that time it was as if I could perceive the answers to everything.

"I understood that I was smaller than the smallest grain of sand on the beach—yet I was also ten thousand feet tall . . . and both at the same time!"

Clint Walker had always believed in God, but now he saw that it was possible for the Creator to permit the soul to inhabit new bodies in different life experiences.

"The body is just a vehicle, a garment that we put on for a while, but the soul goes on forever. It cannot be destroyed."

Clint began to think of all the things that he still wished to accomplish on Earth. "Please, Lord," he prayed, "I want another crack at life."

And then he was back in his body. "Now this leads me to speculate," he said, "if we, ourselves, might possibly determine the time when we die."

Walker has only vague memories of being transported down the hillside in a toboggan and of lying in a hospital three hours later.

"Two doctors had already pronounced me dead," he remembered. "A third doctor just happened to be passing through the room where

I lay, taking a shortcut to somewhere else—and in a glance, he believed that I was still alive. He didn't even take time to wash his hands before he was opening me up."

Then Clint saw himself moving down a long tunnel. There were faces around him that he could not clearly identify. There were voices that he could not distinguish. But Clint asked God to allow him to live.

Afterward, the doctor declared Walker to be a medical miracle.

"You should have died," he told the actor, "or at the very least, have been left a vegetable."

Australian actor Paul Hogan, best known for his portrayal of the colorful outdoorsman in the popular motion picture *Crocodile Dundee*, explained (*Examiner*, February 19, 1991) how he received the idea to portray an angel in a recent film, *Almost an Angel*.

Hogan had been working out in a Sydney, Australia gym when he foolishly tried to see how much weight he could bench press.

"Boom! My head just seemed to *burst*! I'd never felt such intense pain before."

Doctors found that the actor had burst a blood vessel in his brain, and Hogan spent a month in the hospital recovering.

During that time, he overheard some of the staff saying that if they could not reduce his blood pressure, he would be a dead man.

"At one point I thought I was dying," Hogan said. "Half of me was glad, because it meant the terrible pain would stop. But the other half of me said: 'Don't be silly. I'm not ready to go yet!' "

As he would drift in and out of consciousness, he would see the ceiling lift up and he would think that he saw alien creatures from other worlds.

Hogan was fortunate in that the hemorrhage hadn't done any permanent damage, and the doctors told him that such an incident was unlikely to recur.

Surviving the accident had provided him with another plus. He received his inspiration for the film *Almost an Angel,* in which he portrayed a crook who believes himself to have died and come back to life as an angel.

"I drew upon my experience of being in the hospital, hallucinating, and being near death," Hogan said. "Throughout the movie, I try to tell people, 'Don't be too afraid of death. It may not be the end of everything.' "

Explaining that his near-death experience had given him a new outlook on life, Hogan admitted: "I've stopped taking life for granted. I appreciate every new day as it comes along. Now I don't plan too far into the future, and I get greater joy out of the simple things of life."

• 26 •

"Death Is Like Opening the Door to Another Room"

In 1942 the First Marine Division was ashore on Guadalcanal, digging in at Henderson Field against the mounting Japanese attacks on the perimeter.

Sergeant Ted Snowden recalled that they had been under unusually heavy fire for days and that during the worst of the bombardment the ground shook like an earthquake. Some of the marines had been bruised from the vibrations alone, for they were rattled from side to side in their foxholes "like dice in a cup."

At night battleships with fourteen-inch guns shelled them, and the entrenched marines would pray for daylight. When first light came, the

Japanese planes would take over and bomb them until nightfall.

"The rare times when the bombers didn't come and the ships were silent, there was an artillery piece we called 'Pistol Pete' perched on a hill not far away that took potshots at us," Snowden wrote in the November–December 1951, issue of *Fate* magazine.

In spite of the heavy Japanese bombardment, little actual damage was done. All of the important equipment was kept well-hidden in the jungle, and often when a U.S. plane landed it could be successfully refueled in the thick undergrowth even in the face of an attack.

On the particular day when Snowden's remarkable experience occurred, things had been relatively quiet. U.S. aircraft that had been hit in the fighting of the previous day was being repaired, and an air-raid alarm in the morning had produced little damage or injury.

Pistol Pete had begun to take its daily target practice, opening fire here and there, but not seriously affecting the airfield.

The Japanese artillery piece with the colorful nickname was actually a howitzer that fired a high-trajectory low-velocity shell, and it was more of nuisance than a real threat since it seldom hit anything of consequence. Because it traveled so high in the air to get to where it was supposed to be going, it could always be heard—and the marines would simply hit the dirt and hope for it to land far away.

By nightfall of that day, the men were secure in newly dug foxholes. Danger from falling trees the night before had caused them to move their foxholes from the forest onto a grassy meadow. The moon was full, shining down on the embattled men with unpretentious simplicity.

As the men talked among themselves to keep up morale, the whee-whee-whee-whee sound of the howitzer informed them that Pistol Pete was after them again.

A shell exploded one hundred yards from the foxholes, and some of the men grew apprehensive. Pistol Pete was getting too close.

Snowden had hoped that he might be able to get some sleep that night, but Pistol Pete had other plans. Having registered on target, the howitzer proceeded to bombard the Yanks in their foxholes.

"The shells came in regularly," Snowden recalled, "about a minute apart and ranged all through our foxholes."

The men had time after each explosion to rise up and see where it had hit. Shallow craters about eight feet apart were appearing throughout the meadow—some quite close to foxholes with marines in them.

Snowden felt apprehensive. "Pistol Pete had never looked that good before."

As he sought to relax in his foxhole, Sergeant

Snowden heard Pistol Pete's "whee-whee-whee" and suddenly knew with a certainty that this particular shell could not get any closer.

"This is it!" he thought to himself.

The shell came screaming toward him, louder and louder—until the shrill screech had engulfed his entire universe.

Snowden heard the thud into the left side of his foxhole.

Then, suddenly, without knowing how or why it happened, Snowden—*or some part of him*—was standing in the moon-shade of a large tree watching his physical body in the foxhole.

"The outline of my helmet and body was plainly visible to me, as I—or this *other* part of me—stood there waiting for the explosion to wipe the picture away.

"I remember the bright moonlight, the pattern of our foxholes, and the fresh over-pattern of the shell scars. I saw this impression only—as I didn't take my eyes off my body.

"I remember anticipation, but mainly I felt calm—a calm such as I had never known before. It was a calmness that nothing could shake."

Snowden clearly saw the white blast of the explosion and its deadly red core. He watched as his foxhole erupted and widened to the crater of a shell-hole.

All of this his Real Self viewed from a height of about thirty yards; and though he saw it, he neither heard the blast nor felt the heat.

"The next thing I knew, I was back with my body again, lying on my left side, facing what had been the side of the foxhole, but was now only a loose rubble of smoking, hot clods of dirt."

Snowden knew that he was completely exposed except for his back, which was pressed against what remained of the other side of his foxhole.

Miraculously, he had somehow escaped injury.

He made a quick check of legs, arms, back. He felt nothing mangled or destroyed.

But he was aware of a ". . . whirring sensation in the top of my head and a feeling of being cramped for space inside my body."

This restricted sensation, by comparison, brought back a sharp memory of the lightness and freedom that he had experienced while floating outside of his body. Other than that, he seemed to be all right.

"My God, they got the sarge!" he heard a voice shout.

"Like hell they did!" he yelled, without moving. "You men keep your heads down!"

As if to complete some bizarre series of experiences, Snowden never heard another shell that entire night—although it was a matter of record that one of his men caught a splinter in his chest and lung and was evacuated the next morning.

But Snowden never stirred from his foxhole-shell-hole, and he slept peacefully for the rest of the night.

"I still do not understand this incredible experience," Snowden concluded a decade later. "But I do know that it has removed all fear of dying from my mind.

"I now believe death—or transition—is accomplished with far greater ease than the opening of a door into another room."

• 27 •

Her Near-Death Experience
Brought Her to Other Worlds

In August of 1973, after an article about my exploration of the near-death experience appeared in a national publication, I received an interesting letter from Jessie H. of Seattle which described her own adventure between dimensions of reality.

"When I was a 'sick' sixteen, as was my usual self-willed, disobedient wont, I disregarded Mama's pleading and went to school intending to participate in an important swim meet. The Result: *Pleurisy!* An illness which causes restrictive, laborious, painful breathing.

"Mama was beside herself as I screamed for each wisp of air. We had no telephone then, so she sent my brother to Papa's shoe shop and told him to fetch Doc Watkins.

"The first thing that Doc did was cut my pajama top right down the middle and plaster my chest with Denver Mud to reduce the inflammation. Then Doc left, followed by Mama and Papa. My little luminous-dialed Ingersoll said, seven-thirty."

And then, Jessie recalled, *it* happened!

She felt herself begin to leave her physical body.

"I let out a piercing scream, and Mama came running up the stairs. One look at me, and she shrieked, 'Papo! Papo!', which brought Papa bounding up the stairs.

"I'll never forget his horrified face as I looked down on him from my spirit body up near the ceiling, Mama stood behind him moaning, '*Yezhish! Marya! Josefe!*' "

Up near the ceiling, where Jessie continued to hover, she could see her father bending over her, breathing into her mouth.

"I took in Mama's anguish, but I was not a part of the emotional scene below me.

"I shall never forget the peace that I experienced when I was out of my body. I felt a dynamic kind of consciousness of joy and well-being. And I enjoyed the total freedom of locomotion to any point that I desired at an instant's decision.

"I remember feeling sympathy toward Mama and Papa and the pain that attended their deep concern for me, but I did not partake of any of their anxiety.

"I also remember looking at my precious little clock which now said eight-oh-five—and then I *whooshed* back into my body!"

Jessie tried to explain to her parents what had happened to her Real Self, but they shushed her and told her to go to sleep.

"And I never did tell them—or anyone else—about my near-death experience. I didn't want people thinking that I was crazy or odd or peculiar. Thank you for granting me the opportunity to tell you about it. I never thought that I would have such a chance."

Jessie went on to explain that her dramatic near-death experience had apparently opened a doorway for her Soul to travel across the universe.

"I don't know why it seems to be so difficult for so many to accept these kinds of experiences. Why can others not accept the fact that thought, being instantaneous, enables us to catapult ourselves to distant planets almost instantly?"

Jessie admitted that immediately after her illness, when she would begin to feel the "going-out-of-the-body sensation" coming over her physical self, she would "resist it with great fear and screaming." Her cries of distress would always bring her parents to her bedside, and they would comfort her with reassuring words of their proximity.

And, yet, she observed, "experiences that a person is meant to have will not be denied.

"I would awaken in the morning and remember distinctly having traveled infinite distances—navigating and exploring other planets at close range.

"I could perceive vapors on some worlds, thick and wispy like blankets hanging down.

"Sometimes vivid shafts of light streaked out from nebulous matter."

And often in the in-between universes in which she traveled, Jessie heard sounds and sensed "all kinds of activity and life."

She went on to explain that by "life" she meant ". . . the recognition that *something* was watching over me and taking care of me; that is, taking care of my Soul, which I know will be in existence forever.

"And always I had the sense of infinity and eternity—and the awareness that I was an intact entity, eternal and indestructible.

"I believe that there will come a time when humankind will be spiritually evolved to the point that we will be able to chart the universe in just the way that I have described."

· 28 ·

Into the Light

During the summer of 1935, Fay Marvin Clark was involved in a serious automobile accident. As he lay in a hospital bed and stared at the two doctors who were discussing his condition—a condition that he certainly did not consider as being very serious—he realized that he really did not feel any pain at all, only a sense of physical tiredness.

And yet the two medical men talked on and on about how he had been bleeding quite profusely from both ears, and how his skull was fractured and some of his ribs were crushed.

"Soon my mind began to take on a new feeling," Fay wrote in his book, *Into the Light*. "I had a sensation of alertness or awareness that I had never before experienced. The room and each object in it seemed to take on a new sharpness of detail."

Fay remembered that the obvious seriousness of the doctors began to amuse him, because he knew that he could get up at any time and leave the hospital.

But then as his vision sharpened, he realized that he was viewing things from a very different perspective.

He now found himself looking *down* on his body as it lay on the bed, and his point of view seemed to be coming from the ceiling on the other side of the room.

There was no question about it. He was able to see himself lying on the bed *below* him.

It took Fay a bit longer to comprehend that while the physical body on the bed was his, it certainly was not his *true* self.

"Here I was looking down on the entire room with a sharpness of vision and a clearness of perception and understanding that I had never before experienced."

Even his sense of hearing seemed to have sharpened, for he now understood that the two doctors thought that he had died, for they were no longer talking about him, but about similar cases where the patient had *also* died.

How long he lay "dead," Fay did not know. Later, one of the doctors told him that it was possibly five minutes.

While it was strictly against his early religious training to believe in the continued existence of any part of him after the death of his physical body, it was with no sense of fear, but with a fuller understanding, that Fay began to survey his new condition.

He felt freer, more able to perceive his relationship to everything than ever before.

Fay looked down on his body and felt no regret at having left it. Rather, he experienced a sense of release.

"I had a feeling that while it had been a good body and had been valuable to me, I would have no further need of it."

Because he was curious, Fay wondered about the other patients in the hospital.

The first floor contained the emergency room where his body lay. The actual patients' rooms were all on the second floor.

He no sooner thought about the other patients than he found himself on the second floor, mentally opening each door, hoping to find someone to talk with. But in each room, he found only empty beds.

After Fay had visited each room on both sides of the hall and found no one, his thoughts returned to the doctors in the room where his physical body rested. Again, he found himself in his former position, up next to the ceiling, observing his body on the bed and listening to the doctors' conversation.

One of the doctors walked over to the bed, picked up the edge of the sheet, and started to drop it over Fay's face.

"At that instant, I felt myself somehow being drawn to my body, where it lay on the bed. I felt myself entering my body, and the feelings of warmth and freedom left me. I found myself once again in my body, cold, cramped, and restricted of movement. I could only see ahead of me instead of in all directions. I remember hearing the doctor call out that he believed my eyes had moved."

All through the night and for many nights and days to come, that powerful sense of understanding never left him—*we do not die . . . only our physical body dies.*

"The truth of survival after bodily death was so overwhelming and beyond my comprehension that I did not tell the nurse or either of the doctors," Fay said. "In fact, I did not even tell my wife, as I was afraid that even she could not understand what had happened."

When he left the hospital, Fay asked one of the doctors if he really thought that he had died that first night. He replied that by all the rules that he knew, Fay should not be walking out of the hospital.

"You must not have finished your work on Earth," the doctor suggested. "Be thankful. Otherwise you would not be alive."

Two years later, after Fay had shared the

story of his strange experience with each of the doctors and many others, one of them started kidding him that he must not have looked in *all* the rooms on the second floor that night, as they *always* had patients there.

He then called his nurse to check the records for the night that Fay was admitted to the hospital. To his astonishment, the nurse returned with the records that that had been one of the few nights ever that there had been *no* patients on the second floor!

That near-death experience back in 1935 was the activating incident that started Fay M. Clark on a quiet search for knowledge and the Truth that led him around the world and exposed him to many cultures and philosophies.

Fay became one of my early mentors, and his guidance and encouragement was greatly beneficial to my development as an author and a researcher. The years that we spent exploring the unknown together are among the richest and most rewarding of my life experience. His counsel and advice was always balanced, practical, and down-to-earth—in spite of the other-worldly subjects which we pursued and studied.

During numerous controlled experiments, Fay returned in essence to the in-between universe of near-death. Here are a few of his conclusions after years of study and exploration:

"After the separation from the physical body at so-called death, one finds himself awake and in the astral world. He or she will find that no one is punished by nature or by God. People punish themselves by their own misbehavior or ignorance."

"There are those entities who choose to stay on the astral plane to give encouragement and assistance to those who have just passed over. Those giving assistance to newcomers to the astral plane add greatly to their own growth by so doing."

"The astral body is the seat of feeling, passion, desires, and emotion; and like our physical body, it is only a temporary housing for our entity or eternal spiritual self."

"Theosophists hold that no sudden change takes place in man upon physical death. He will remain exactly what he was before. He will retain the same intellect, virtues, and vices. *The only change will be that he no longer has a physical body.* The surroundings and conditions in which he will find himself are those which his own thoughts and desires have already created for him."

"Usually life on the astral plane so closely resembles a continuation of Earth life that many newcomers to the astral plane fail to realize that they actually passed through a physical death experience.

"Most Christians and members of many other religious systems believe in the immortality of the soul. They expect a continuation of life after death—and this is exactly what happens, using the astral body that lives on independent of the physical body.

"It is claimed that the astral world consists of a series of planes created by the different rates of vibratory energy. The ancient metaphysicians referred to the presence of at least seven planes of existence of which our physical world is one.

"None of these planes are supernatural. They are all within—and operating according to—the Laws of Nature. They may be supernormal to most persons, but as we evolve, they will become more and more normal to each of us. Each plane is not a place, but a state of being."

"I believe in the Oneness of all Life. I believe that all life, all forms of matter, are a part of the Creator that humankind has called upon throughout the ages. I believe that this Creator is not a physical being, but that it is a form of intelligent energy, force, or mind—and that this force or mind is neither vengeful nor vindictive. I believe that the goal of this intelligence, force, or mind is the evolution of a perfect universe—

which, of course, also includes the perfection of humankind."

Fay Marvin Clark made his final transition on October 23, 1990.

• 29 •

Manifestations of the Spirit Body at the Moment of Death or Near-Death Experiences

"I am the pilot of ever-evolving life—often mistakenly called Terrible Death. I am thy brother, uplifter, redeemer, friend—unloader of thy gross burden of body troubles. I come to fetch thee away from the valley of thy broken dreams to a wondrous highland of light, to which poison vapors of sorrow cannot climb."
Paramahansa Yogananda

Whenever a parapsychologist or a psychical researcher is asked to describe the areas of human experience that present the most favorable climate for psychic phenomena, he or she will be certain to include, somewhere near the top of the list, the point of death.

Dr. Gardner Murphy once commented that death is the most obvious situation which appears to precipitate psychic phenomena, although he also includes ". . . severe illness, things that are either biologically or in a broad sense personal crises—disrupting, alerting situations that we have to be ready for, capable of assimilating, warding off, or that call for defense or the ability to incorporate . . ."

Among the most common and universal of all psychic phenomena is that of the "crisis apparition," that ghostly image which is seen, heard, or felt when the individual represented by the image is undergoing a severe physical crisis—especially that of death.

It would appear, judging by such cases as those that we have examined in this book, that at the moment of physical death, the soul, the essential self in all persons, is emancipated from the confines of the body and is able to soar free of time and space—and in some instances, is able to make a last, fleeting contact with a loved one. These projections at the moment of death or near-death experiences betoken that *something* nonphysical exists within the human organism that is capable of making mockery of accepted physical laws and, even more importantly, is capable of surviving physical death.

The ghostly visitor that is known as a crisis apparition looks and acts just like the actual physical personality that it represents, and its principal function and sole motivation appears to be its desire to say good-bye to a relative or a friend.

Professor Ian Currie, a former lecturer in anthropology and sociology at Guelph University in Ontario, Canada, and author of the book, *You Cannot Die,* shared the following cases with writer Joe Mullins:

Early one morning a U.S. serviceman who was stationed in Germany showed up quite unexpectedly at his family home in a Detroit suburb.

His mother, who was startled in the act of preparing breakfast, was overjoyed to set another plate for her son.

"Sorry, Mom," he said, declining the meal with a gentle smile. "I can't stay for breakfast. I just wanted to say good-bye."

The young soldier waved farewell and walked out the door.

His heartbroken mother ran after him, shouting for him to return and stay longer—but she saw that he had completely disappeared.

A few hours later, an officer appeared at their door to inform the family that their beloved son had been killed in a training accident 6,000 miles away in Germany—just a half an hour before his mysterious visit.

In another case from Professor Currie's files, it seems that two friends went into partnership in a Boston clothing store, but one later skipped town with all of their money.

In spite of the one partner's treachery, the business went on to prosper.

Half a dozen or so years later, the owner of the clothing store was stunned when his old friend and former partner walked in the door.

The prodigal partner waved aside all amenities and got immediately to the point of his visit. He said that he had come back to apologize and to say that he was sorry for what he had done.

The successful businessman embraced his old friend and said that he forgave him.

The long-lost friend's face brightened at once. "Thank you," he said, then quickly left the store.

It was several days before the businessman learned that his ex-partner had died the morning of his sudden visit—just three hours *before* he walked into the store to ask forgiveness.

Some years ago when I was appearing on a radio show over CKTB, St. Catherine, Ontario, a young woman called in with a most interesting account of a crisis apparition. Her voice quavered with emotion as she related the experience that had provided her with her own proof of survival.

She had been sleeping one night for just a few hours when she was awakened by the form of her brother standing at the foot of the bed.

"I'm sorry, sis, for all the trouble that I may have caused you. I love you," he told her.

Her husband awakened at the interruption of his sleep, but by the time that he had blinked his eyes into full consciousness, the image of his brother-in-law had disappeared.

His wife insisted that she had truly seen her brother standing in their bedroom, and she described in detail what he had been wearing. She had particularly noticed that he was wearing a plaid shirt that she had never before seen him wear.

No sooner had she completed her description of the apparition when the telephone rang, and the woman was given the tragic news that her brother had been killed in an automobile accident.

Later, when they visited the morgue to identify the body, both of them were startled to see the corpse attired in a plaid shirt such as the one that she had described.

The phenomena of the crisis apparition is as universal as death itself, and its pattern is almost exact enough to comprise a consistent formula:

A percipient, either preparing for bed or going about an ordinary workaday task, is suddenly and unexpectedly confronted by the image of a loved one—very often one who the percipient knows is far away.

The apparition is clearly identified as that of

the beloved, and the ghostly visitor often gives some sign of parting or affection.

Within a very short period of time after the apparition has faded from view, the percipient receives word that the loved one—whose image he or she has just seen—has passed from life to death—or near-death.

• 30 •

His Spirit Self Brought Help to Rescue His Physical Body

A man who I shall call Ross figured in a case of NDE in which the spirit self was able to communicate a telepathic plea for help to a close friend.

Ross was alone in a fourteen-foot trench, welding some new water pipes for a soon-to-open housing development in a large New England city.

It is quite unlikely that Ross had ever given the slightest thought to any sort of extrasensory or spiritual abilities, either in himself or in others.

And if anyone had told him that he might travel in his spirit self, totally independent of his physical body, he would more than likely have laughed in his face.

Ross had a wife and six children to support. He worked on a city maintenance crew from 7:30 A.M. to 4:00 P.M., and he held down a second job as a garage attendant from 7:30 P.M. to midnight. He didn't have any spare minutes to devote to far-out discussions of metaphysics or religion.

Then on a late afternoon in the spring of 1955, Ross was given a most dramatic, albeit painful, demonstration that he had within himself remarkable resources which lay ready to serve him in a crisis situation.

By 3:30 P.M. the power-shovel crew had laid the last pipe in place for the day. At 4:00 P.M. the crew knocked off work for the day.

On that particular afternoon, however, Ross did not have to report for work at the garage, so he decided to pick up some overtime by finishing the welding on the seam between the last two pipes in the trench.

He had finished his work on the inside seam and was about to begin on the outside of the joint when all of a sudden tons of earth, clay, and stones fell upon him.

Ross had had absolutely no warning of any kind. The trench had caved in on him as silently as if it had intended to trap him.

Ross was knocked down in a kneeling position

against the big pipe. His nose was crunched up against the plate of the welding mask.

For a few awful moments, he was conscious of searing pain as his right shoulder was pressed against the hot weld that he had been making on the pipes. In agony, he tried desperately to squirm away from the scalding pipe, but the press of the cave-in held his shoulder fast against the red-hot weld.

Ross tried to twist his face free of the welding mask—but then he realized that it had saved his life. Without the pocket which the mask had made around his face, the loose dirt would have covered his nose and mouth and he would surely have suffocated within a matter of minutes.

He lay very still, taking stock of his situation.

He had been covered by a landslide in a trench in a new housing district.

He was alone. His crew had gone home.

There were no other construction workers or carpenters working on this side of the district, but chances were pretty strong that someone might have occasion to walk by the trench and notice the cave-in.

But even if someone did notice the cave-in, how would they see *him*? How would they know that there was a workman under the pile of rubble?

The terrible thought that no one would discover him until it was much too late dug into his consciousness and began to slice away at the thin mental barrier that had thus far kept him from panic.

It was at that moment that Ross realized for the first time that his right hand was sticking up through the dirt! Somehow, when the force of the cave-in had smashed against him, his right shoulder had been pressed forward against the hot weld and his right arm had been straightened back and above his body, thus allowing his hand to remain above the surface like a lonely five-fingered flag. His right hand could be his salvation!

Time quickly became a concept devoid of all real meaning. How long had he been trapped by the cave-in? Hours, days, weeks?

Stop it! Ross scolded himself. How long *really*?

Perhaps four, five minutes.

But already it was becoming difficult to breathe. He had been very fortunate that he had been forced up against the large pipe, thereby creating large air pockets near him.

But the blood from his broken nose kept dripping into his throat, and he feared that he would eventually choke to death on it.

Would no one ever come?

Ross thought of his wife, his children—and he was startled by the vividness of his thoughts. It seemed as if each member of his family had suddenly entered into the trench to be near him in his agony.

"The more I thought about my family," he remembered, "the more I wanted to be with them one last time.

"Each breath I was taking was beginning to feel like hot lead being forced down my nostrils.

"The next thing I knew, I seemed somehow to be floating above the trench. I thought that I had died.

"I could see my right hand kind of drooping down over a bit of my wrist sticking above the dirt, but I didn't really seem to care any longer what had happened to me. I didn't even feel sad. Just kind of indifferent.

"Then I thought of my family—and just like that, I was there in the kitchen. My wife was peeling potatoes for the evening meal. Our oldest girl was helping her.

"I walked through the house and saw each one of the kids. Some were watching television. Others were doing homework.

"I wanted so much to hug them one last time. I wanted them to see me.

"That's when I felt sad.

"That's when I knew that I didn't want to die.

"I was discovering that it didn't hurt to die, but I just didn't want to leave my wife and our kids."

Ross managed to "float" back into the kitchen, and he got up right next to his wife's shoulder.

"I tried to scream in her ear that I needed help. But she just couldn't hear me."

Ross reached out to touch her; and whether or not it was coincidence, she jerked around with a surprised look on her face. But he just couldn't get through to her.

Then Ross thought of Buzz, his best friend and another welder.

"I no sooner pictured him in my mind than I was there beside him. I could see his wristwatch, because he had his shirtsleeves rolled up. It was four-forty-five, which meant that I had been in the caved-in trench about fifteen minutes.

"Buzz works for a commercial firm, not the city, so I knew that he would be working until five o'clock or after, depending on the job.

"Welding work becomes kind of automatic after a while, so I could see Buzz just welding away, not really thinking about much of anything."

And then Ross made the astonishing discovery that he could actually hear what Buzz was thinking.

"His thoughts were all jumbled-up, like in a dream. I suppose that he was kind of daydreaming—and maybe that's how I was able to get through to him!"

Ross reached out in his spirit body and tapped his friend on the shoulder.

"Buzz shut off the torch and lifted up his face mask.

"While I kind of seemed to have his attention, I thought just as hard as I could: 'Buzz! This is Ross! I need your help!' "

Ross was thrilled when he saw Buzz open his eyes wide, like he had seen a ghost.

"He said my name out loud in kind of a hoarse voice, and Artie, who was working with him, asked him what was going on.

" 'It was the weirdest thing,' Buzz said. 'I thought I saw Ross standing in front of me.'

"Artie told him that he must be seeing things, but I just kept directing my thoughts at Buzz to come looking for me.

"And then I prayed, 'Oh, God, dear God! Please help Buzz to come looking for me!' "

The next thing Ross knew, he was dimly aware of the sensation of some hands grasping at him and pulling at him. As if from very far away, he could hear a lot of excited voices—and above them all, he could hear Buzz saying, "Be gentle. Hey, take it easy!"

At first Ross was still confused.

"I didn't know if I was still floating around the place like some kind of ghost—or if I was really back in my body and being rescued from the cave-in.

"Mostly, I felt scared, because I thought that maybe my mind was playing tricks with me—and that *now* I really was dead.

"Then a wonderful kind of peace came over me, and when I woke up again, I was in the hospital and all my family was standing around me. That's when I really knew that Buzz had heard my cry for help and that I had been rescued—and I was still alive!"

Ross was greatly impressed with the authenticity of his experience. He had never before been concerned with such things as near-death experiences, nor had he ever read any literature that had dealt with psychic or spiritual occurrences. Now he is completely convinced that a man and his mind are more than physical things.

His friend Buzz was quite vocal concerning his view of the experience. He said that when he had looked up from his welding, he had at first thought that his eyes had not yet adjusted from dealing with the bright light of the welding torch. Although a welder wears a tinted faceplate in his helmet, he is still very susceptible to afterimages.

When he was convinced that his eyes were not playing tricks on him, he was certain that he could distinguish a misty outline of his best friend Ross, standing before him.

"I also received a very strong sense of danger," Buzz explained further. "And I was motivated to leave my work at once. Somehow I knew that I must drive to the housing development where I knew Ross was working with his crew. Although I knew that he should have quit work nearly an hour before, I was convinced that he was for some reason still there and that he needed my help real bad."

Buzz admitted that he has had a number of experiences which he considers to have been psychic or spiritual in nature. He firmly believes in the immortality of the human soul, and he is convinced that after death a person's spirit, or spiritual essence, survives physical death.

Buzz had a prior experience similar to that of perceiving the "living ghost" of his friend Ross. Seven years before, Buzz's sister had appeared to him at the moment of her physical death in another state.

It would appear, then, that Buzz had served as just precisely the proper receiver for Ross's telepathic cry for help—and Ross was indeed fortunate to have a friend who was so readily able to "tune in" to an out-of-body distress call.

· 31 ·

The Power of Prayer Summoned Her to Her Mother's Deathbed

Mary Kennedy has experienced a number of unusual occurrences in her life, but the one that she will always remember as most remarkable is when her mother's dying prayers summoned her to her bedside for one final farewell.

It was on Valentine's Day of 1977. Mary, her husband Brian, and her daughter Kim were staying with her husband's sister and brother-in-law, Betty and Joe Frampton, in Louisville, Kentucky. Mary was tired after the day's activities, and she decided against going to the movies with her husband and nephew.

She retired early, but awoke when Brian returned. "What time is it?" she asked.

Brian checked his watch. "It's ten-twenty-five."

Mary made a mental note of this figure, rolled over, and went back to sleep.

It seemed as if she had just turned over when she suddenly saw an old man with a long white beard dressed in a dark robe standing by her bedside.

"The walls seemed to have disappeared," Mary said, "and it was as if I could see the outdoors. The old man in the robe looked down at me for a moment, then he reached out his hand to me and said 'Come.' "

She spoke not a word, but placed her hand in his.

"I rose from the bed and went with him without question. I glanced down and saw that my nightgown had disappeared, and in its place was a flowing white robe.

"I knew that the night air was cold, but I was oblivious to it. The old man and I were floating just above the treetops. The sky was filled with stars, and below I could see the lights of towns and cities."

After they had traveled like this for a period of time, Mary saw that they were coming closer to the ground, just barely skimming above the sidewalk of some small town.

She looked around, seeking some identifying clue as to where they might be. Then she spied a large plateglass window with the name JAMESON in large red letters.

Immediately she knew where she was. The window was part of the mining company's store in the small Kentucky town where she had grown up.

A few houses and turns later, and she and the old man were moving up the steps to her brother Al's house.

The porch was small, and there was a swing, filling up what little space there was. Unavoidably, the two travelers brushed against the swing as they passed, and it struck the wall of the house with a thud.

"The old man in the robe opened the door slightly for me to enter, then he disappeared," Mary said.

As she stepped into the room and looked around, she could see her father, brother, and sister-in-law Lucille. Her sister Margaret was standing near the stairway at the back side of the room. Her brother's five-year-old son was sitting on the second step of the stair in his pajamas. Several friends and neighbors were also in the room, as well as a few folks unknown to her.

"I walked to the foot of a bed that stood in the center of the room by the front window. In the bed lay my mother, who opened her eyes and smiled at me."

"Thank God," Mary heard her mother say. "I knew you'd come."

"I wanted so very much to talk to Mama," Mary said. "But even though I could see and hear everything going on in the room, I didn't seem to be able to say a word. And no one except Mama seemed to be able to see me."

"Mary," her mother told her, "I wanted to see you so bad, that I begged God to send you to me before I died. Don't you grieve none. I'm going to rest. I'll be waiting for you."

Mary recalled that although her mother looked frail and weak, she suddenly found the energy to rise into a sitting position in her bed.

"I'm so happy to see you," her mother said. "Always remember to ask God when you need help. He'll never fail you. Now I can die happy."

After her mother had spoken those words, she fell back on the bed.

"A man dressed in a brown overcoat and a brown hat went to Mama's bed, felt her pulse, and pulled the sheet up over her head. 'She's dead,' he said in a low voice. I looked up at the clock and saw that it was ten-thirty."

The room dissolved into the confusion of the aftermath of the death of a loved one.

"My brother Al was so close to me as he went out the door that I could have touched him," Mary said. "But I knew that he would not be able to feel me."

Everyone in the room began to weep. Mary's

sister Margaret fainted, and some neighbors took her to their home so that she might be revived in solitude.

"And then all at once I saw my mother's body lying on something that looked like an ironing board with two men bending over it. I got really upset and agitated about this—although I didn't really know why," Mary said.

"The men were doing something to Mama's body—what I could not see. Whatever it was, though, I knew that I had to stop it.

"I tried to jerk the arm of one man away from Mama's body, but it was evident that I could not be felt. I could not utter a sound, and I could not make my physical presence known. To my deep sadness, I was unable to restrain the two men from doing whatever it was that they were doing to Mama."

And then she was back in bed in Louisville.

"My husband's sister Betty was washing my face with a cold washcloth, and Brian had my head and shoulders in his arms," Mary said. "My nightgown was wet with sweat, and my hair was damp from it. I was very cold and weak. But the first thing I asked when I was able to speak was the time. It was ten-thirty-five."

Mary Kennedy immediately informed her husband and sister-in-law that her mother was dead. She told them that she had seen her die at ten-thirty.

"No one believed me. I was told that I had just had a bad nightmare.

"Brian said that he had been sitting at the edge of the bed, having a last cigarette before going to bed, when I had begun to moan. Large drops of sweat had formed on my face, and he had called Betty to help rouse me."

Mary was convinced that her mother was dead and that word would come the following morning.

It was three days before word came.

"I went to the post office and there was a letter from my brother Al: "We tried to get you, sis, before Mom died. She died on Valentine's Day evening at ten-thirty, and we kept her as long as possible. We buried her this evening."

The letter was postmarked the day before.

The next morning as Mary prepared to travel to her hometown—by more conventional means this time—she received a telegram from the post office:

"Mom got pneumonia. Not expected to live. Come at once."

Mary said that she would always feel that pain. "For some reason the telegram had been delayed in mailing, and it had arrived too late for me to see Mama alive."

When Mary Kennedy arrived in the small Kentucky mining town where she had been born and reared, she found that her sister-in-law Lucille had cleaned the room in which Mama had died, even to the extent of removing the bed and rearranging the furniture.

Before she would let any of them tell her anything, Mary asked her brother to call in a neighbor who she knew well and who she knew had been present the night of her mother's death.

"I then related my remarkable experience," Mary said. "And to verify it, I told them where everyone in the room had been seated or standing and exactly how the furniture had been arranged that night."

When Mary completed her amazing account, Lucille showed her two boards lying in the backyard. Nailed together, they resembled a crude ironing board. The deceased woman had been prepared for burial in the house, and the boards had been used by the undertakers for the embalming process.

Then Mary was able to understand her feelings of disgust toward the men that she had tried to keep from her mother in the strange vision.

"Mama had a horror of being embalmed, and once she had made me promise that if I was present when she died, I would not let her body be embalmed."

Al and Lucille told Mary that Mama had told all those present that she would be able to die happy if she could only see Mary one last time.

"Mama had prayed all day that I'd come. Al and Lucille said that just before Mama died, something had hit the front porch swing and it had struck the wall with a loud thud. Right after that, something had opened the front door, even though it was a clear frosty night and no breeze was stirring. Al had closed the door just after Mama had died.

"They told me, too, that just before Mama had died, she suddenly sat up in bed and had passed away while she was smiling and talking—while looking straight at the foot of the bed. They could catch a word here and there, but thought that she was delirious."

"Did my mother really see me in answer to her dying prayers?" Mary asked.

"Did my soul leave my body to go out to be with the one who was preparing to take flight to Heaven so that she could die happy?

"I believe so," she concluded.

• 32 •

Astral Flight and Bilocation from a Doomed Train

William McFarland Campbell was a traveling insurance man with the Canadian Order of Chosen Friends for more than thirty years. In his position of Grand Organizer, he traveled from coast to coast from his home base of Hamilton, Ontario.

In 1910, Campbell was ready to retire when a boom hit the northern Ontario town of Sudbury. Nickel had been discovered in large quantities and people from all walks of life were streaming into the little town. Consequently, forgetting about early retirement, Campbell often found himself waiting for the train to take him to Sudbury and back home to Hamilton.

It was January 21, 1910. Train Number 17

arrived on time, and Campbell joined the other passengers for the half-block walk to the platform. With their suitcases in hand, the men and women swung aboard the train with no knowledge of what lay in store for them.

A rail lay broken at a point north of Toronto on the Soo Branch of the track where the Canadian Pacific Railway crosses the Spanish River at the eastern approach to an iron bridge. Before the engineer could even realize what was happening, the first-class car was off the tracks, plummeting down the icy river below. With the first-class car came the dining car and the sleeping car, both pulled inexorably along. These cars pulled the second-class car with them—and then car after wooden car toppled over the embankment into the icy gorge below. As the cars tumbled over and over into the river, they left splintered wood and mangled bodies scattered over the wintry scene.

That night Mary Campbell sat up late, waiting for her husband to come home. The clock on the mantel struck 10:00 P.M., and she folded the last bit of sewing she had been working on and placed it in her basket. In another hour, Will would be home.

At eleven o'clock, Mary turned up the gas lamp and rested her feet on the stool by her chair.

As she waited, she heard the sound of a taxi coming down the street. It turned on Grant

Avenue and slowly passed the houses of their neighbors.

At last she heard it stop at their house, and the driver call out a "good night."

She heard Will's unmistakable step on the front porch.

Mary came forward, opened the door and welcomed her husband home.

But she frowned when she saw that Will's hat was pulled down low over his eyes, and his face was averted from hers.

"What's wrong, Will?" she wanted to know at once. "Did things not go well today?"

When he finally lifted his face, Mary could not halt a shriek of horror from escaping her mouth.

Her beloved husband's face was transparent. His eyes were two glowing coals.

Will was struggling to speak, but he could only manage an unpleasant gurgling sound.

Mary's frightened cries awakened the neighbors and brought them to her aid.

She was huddled on the floor when they found her, and it was evident that she was in an advanced state of shock.

When one of the neighbors answered the insistently ringing telephone, he learned of the terrible wreck of Number 17.

The following morning Mary Campbell managed to tell her story of Will's ghostly appearance to their family physician, Dr. John Bell. Dr. Bell nodded in sympathy.

"Sometimes when we have lived our lives together with someone, we become so attached to that person that we can recognize immediately when danger is at hand to threaten our loved one. Some believe that there is an aura, a body of energy, surrounding a person that is able to transmit thoughts or warnings—even at a distance," he explained.

After Dr. Bell had administered a sedative to Mary and saw that it was taking effect, he prepared to leave. Although he had provided the distraught woman with a "scientific" explanation for the apparition that she had claimed to have seen of her husband the night before, he did not really believe for one minute that Will Campbell had actually manifested before his wife.

As he was leaving the Campbell residence, however, he spotted Will's old hat on the rack in the hallway. He picked it up, feeling a sudden burden of sorrow. Will Campbell had been a fine man and a good friend.

"Poor Will," Dr. Bell reflected sadly. "He'll never wear this again."

As he turned the hat over in his hands, he saw the pink ticket in the hatband.

Once he had read the wording on the ticket, his face turned ashen gray.

No matter how many times he read and reread the ticket, it still said, TRAIN NUMBER 17, FIRST-CLASS RETURN, SUDBURY, JANUARY 21, 1910.

How could a dead man ride home on a train that did not return? And how could he leave his hat behind in a house that would lay forever beyond his physical reach?

Dr. Bell's brain spun inside his skull, and he had to sit down on a sturdy chair to contemplate the mystery further.

Train Number 17 had been derailed before it had reached Sudbury. Was it possible for a ghost man to ride home on a ghost train?

No application of Dr. Bell's prized scientific procedure could adequately answer such an enigma, but Mary Campbell and all of their family and friends were overjoyed when William Campbell arrived home—in the flesh—on the wrecker the next day.

Will explained that he had been in the first-class car that had struck the bridge and had begun to burn. Somehow his body had been thrown clear during the impact of the collision, and he had been tossed out of the car into below-zero weather. He knew that he had been unconscious for several minutes, and when he returned to a kind of dazed state of semiconsciousness, he sat for several more minutes thinking of his wife and wondering if he would ever see her again.

Later, he roused himself, and set about rendering assistance to other injured passengers.

Will, too, was nonplussed by the story that

Mary told him—and he could never get over his amazement at the mute evidence of the return ticket stub in his hat. Somehow, Will Campbell had managed to be in two places at once!

• 33 •

"Tell Them I'm Still Alive!"

D r. Harry M. Archer was a respected surgeon and medical officer in New York City
around the turn of the century. For a period of
more than thirty years, this remarkable man was
on the scene of every major fire in the city,
rendering assistance both to fire victims and
injured firemen. In 1912, he was awarded the
Fire Department Medal in appreciation of his
services to the city, and he later received the
most coveted civic award of all, the James Gor-
den Bennett Medal.

Writer Frank B. Copley decided that Dr. Archer would make an excellent subject for a fea-
ture article, and the August 8, 1925 issue of
Collier's magazine carried his testament to the

many experiences and colorful reminiscenes of the selfless medical man.

One of the most unusual experiences that Dr. Archer shared took place during a fire in 1920. He resisted trying to explain exactly what had occurred, but he commented that it ". . . seemed to exhale an eerie suggestion of the supernatural."

It was seven-thirty, a cold Sunday night in the city, and a fire had been reported in a rag shop on New York's Lower East Side. From an adjacent tenement, positioned on the fire escape, a group of firemen were training a fire hose onto the blazing five-story structure next door.

The fire escape was only a short distance from a third-floor window of the rag shop, so at about eleven, the lieutenant with the five men on the fire escape, plus members of Engine Company 32, were ordered to take their hose into the building through the window across from them.

This order proved to be a costly error. Within a half an hour after entering the doomed building, the firemen outside on the street heard a series of cracks and snaps followed by a tremendous roar. Within another few seconds, the interior of the building had collapsed, burying the hapless firefighters inside.

The lieutenant and two of his men were rescued almost at once, and they were brought to safety after having sustained only slight injuries.

A large contingent of firemen organized an extensive search through the smoldering rubble and ruins, but hours later, no trace of the three missing men could be found.

By two o'clock in the morning, it was decided that there could be little hope of finding the men alive and word was sent to their families, notifying them of the tragedy.

Dr. Harry Archer had been on the scene to treat the injuries of the survivors, and as was customary for him, he considered it his duty to remain on location until the last man had been recovered—alive or dead.

About an hour later, one of the firemen approached Dr. Archer with a request.

"It's Johnny Seufert's wife, doc. She's at the police line carrying on something dreadful and making a terrible fuss. Do you think you could help her out?"

Dr. Archer gave the fireman a quick nod of his head and went immediately in search of the distressed woman, whose husband could only be dead by this time.

"Dr. Archer!" she cried when she sighted the famous physician. "You'll believe me, I know you will! You've got to make them listen to me. The others don't believe me, but I'm telling the truth."

He took the woman gently by the arm and walked with her a short distance away from the police line. "Please tell me how I may assist you, my dear lady."

"It's not me," she protested. "It's Johnny! Just before I got the telephone message telling me about the accident and that Johnny was lost, Johnny *himself* came to me."

Dr. Archer merely nodded in sympathy, uncertain exactly what the proper response might be to such a statement. Still, the woman did not seem hysterical or in shock.

"I'm telling you the truth," she insisted. "I saw him as plain as could be."

Before he could interject any kind of comment, she continued more resolutely than before.

"Johnny said, 'I'm a way down in the ruins of the fallen building. There are tons of stuff over me. They think I'm dead—but I'm not! Tell them not to let up until they find me. *Tell them I'm still alive. Tell them I'm not dead!'* "

Mrs. Seufert could not be swayed. "Doctor, I tell you Johnny is alive! I know he is. Don't let them stop. Tell them to keep digging and looking through the ruins. They can get my Johnny out. They *have* to get him out!"

And she resolved to cling tenaciously to her ground until they did find her husband.

At ten the following morning, the searching firemen did find another body. It was not Johnny Seufert.

At two that afternoon another body was discovered. Again, it was not Seufert.

Each time a body was brought outside the charred building, Dr. Archer tried to convince Mrs. Seufert to go home. She was in an extremely agitated state, and the doctor knew that if her husband's body ever was finally recovered, it would not be a pleasant sight.

But Mrs. Seufert steadfastly refused to move.

After hours of fruitless searching, a crew of firemen came upon a long piece of pipe sticking up through the debris. Thirty-six hours had now passed since the building had collapsed, but one of the men thought that he had heard a tapping sound coming from the pipe.

They listened for a moment, then picked up a pattern to the tapping: three taps—pause; two taps—pause.

Three . . . two. Three . . . two. *Thirty two!*

That was the number of Johnny Seufert's engine company.

The exhausted rescue team shed their weariness by responding to the need of a fellow firefighter . . . a fellow human.

The men listened once more as the signal was repeated. It was unmistakable.

Dr. Archer picked his way through the charred debris until he stood directly in front of the pipe. He placed his mouth over it and shouted: "Seufert! Is that you?"

"Yes," came the barely audible reply.

"Are you all right?" Dr. Archer shouted again.

"You bet," came the answer. "I am now!"

* * *

It was later learned that Seufert had fallen into a hole of a few feet's depth just before the collapse of the burning building. It had been the pipe with its twisted end that had saved him, for it had bent over in the fall of the building; and as a consequence, no flaming debris had been able to suffocate the trapped man below. The pipe had kept Seufert supplied with air and had proved to be the physical agent that had saved his life.

But what of the nonphysical agent that had rescued Johnny Seufert? What of his image that had appeared to his wife and insisted that he was still alive, trapped beneath the rubble of the collapsed building?

It took two hours for the rescue team to free him. Finally rescued from the tons of debris, Seufert fell into the arms of his wife.

Miraculously, he had received few injuries, his largest discomfort having come from the cramping of his legs in the hole.

Dr. Archer gave him a quick physical examination, then asked about the incredible story that Mrs. Seufert had told. It had been her firm insistence that she had seen his living ghost and that this specter had insisted that the physical Johnny was still alive that was even more instrumental in saving his life than the fortuitous bending of a metal pipe.

How, Dr. Archer wanted to know, had he

managed to leave his body and appear before his wife miles away from the scene of his physical entombment?

The only explanation that Johnny Seufert could offer was that he had just kept thinking about his wife—and about the seemingly impossible fact that for some reason he was still alive when by all logic he should have been dead.

• 34 •

Where Was Admiral Tyron?

On the last night of his life, Admiral George Tyron was seen in two places. While you may suggest that this is by no means remarkable, consider the fact that the two places in question were 1,500 miles apart.

On the night of June 22, 1893, Lady Tyron, wife of Sir George Tyron, K.C.B., noted sailor and fleet tactician, commander-in-chief of Her Britannic Majesty's Mediterranean Squadron, was entertaining in the drawing room of London's Eaton Place. Fashionable ladies and distingished cigar-smoking gentlemen chatted with each other and mingled about the room.

In the midst of this polite social scene, an elderly guest rushed up to Lady Tyron and rather breathlessly asked a most peculiar question: "My dear, is Sir George here?"

Lady Tyron responded with a chuckle. "Why, of course not. You know my husband is with his fleet in the Mediterranean."

The dowager turned in the direction of the drawing room with a puzzled look on her face. "That's what I thought, dear; but my husband insisted that he saw Sir George in the drawing room."

Lady Tyron graciously dismissed the elderly woman's confusion until another of her guests soon approached her with the same absurd question.

And then there was another. And another.

Although it was physically impossible, numerous guests claimed to have encountered Sir George Tyron on that June night in London.

On that same date, off the coast of Asia Minor, eight battleships and five cruisers under the command of Vice-Admiral Sir George Tyron, were sailing from Beirut to Tripoli. It was customary for Her Majesty's Navy to practice maneuvers even in routine fleet movements, and such was the plan for the day. Sir George had recently recovered from an illness, but when he called his subordinates together aboard the flagship *Victoria* to discuss the coming manuevers, he insisted that he had regained his health.

"The ships will sail in parallel columns," he instructed his officers. "Upon signal they will turn and reverse course, each column turning in toward the other. One more turn will bring us into the harbor of Tripoli."

The instructions were explicit. The columns were to be separated by a distance of six cables, or 1,200 yards.

When Maurice Bourke, Sir George's flag captain, heard the orders, he became quite anxious. He pointed out to his superior that both the *Victoria* and the *Camperdown*, the leader of the other column, would require 1,600 to 1,800 yards to complete their turns.

"Begging your pardon, sir," Captain Bourke said, "but if we turn at 1,200 yards, we will surely collide!"

Sir George nodded his agreement. "Yes, Captain Bourke, you are quite correct. The distance stipulated should be eight cables [1,600 yards]."

However, when the signal flags for the column formation were hoisted, Sir George called the flag lieutenant to his side and ordered him to keep the distance at six cables. He even handed the lieutenant a note with the number six written on it.

When Captain Bourke saw the signal hoisted by the flag lieutenant, he reiterated his protest and reminded the admiral of their previous discussion. But Sir George cut him off sharply and repeated his command to "leave it at six cables."

Eleven ships immediately acknowledged the flag lieutenant's signals, but Rear Admiral Markham, in command of the *Camperdown* and the parallel column, anxiously computed the distance between his ship and the *Victoria* and gave his order to hoist the flags halfway—a signal to Sir George that the order had been received but that the ship was not ready to execute it.

Rear Admiral Markham called for the semaphore and asked the *Victoria* if there had not been an error made in computations.

But before his message had even been completed, an impatient signal came from Admiral Tyron: "Why are you not ready to obey my orders?"

Rather than risk the wrath of his superior, Admiral Markham, attempting to quiet his inner dread, signaled that he was now ready to proceed.

Sir George then gave the signal for the execution of his command.

Long before the ships began to turn, it was apparent to all experienced seamen that the *Victoria* and the *Camperdown* were bound to crash into each other.

Captain Bourke tried once again in vain to alert Sir George of the inevitability of the impending collision. But Tyron seemed beset by a strange lassitude, and he made no response to the captain's entreaties.

In desperation, Bourke ordered a midshipman to relay the distance to the *Camperdown*, hoping that he might be able to rouse Rear Admiral Markham to action.

Although he observed Captain Bourke's defiance of his direct orders, Sir George simply glanced around him, a bemused expression on his face.

The two ships were terrifyingly near when Captain Bourke asked permission to reverse the port engine.

He received no reply from Sir George.

Only on Captain Bourke's third request did the admiral flutter a dismissive hand and mumble, "Yes, yes, do so."

Bourke threw all caution aside and assumed control of the ship, taking additional steps on his own responsibility in an attempt to save his vessel and the lives of his men.

Meanwhile, on board the *Camperdown*, Rear Admiral Markham had finally decided to take similar desperate tactics.

But it was too late.

With a sickening sound of ripping metal, the 10,000-ton *Camperdown* rammed into the side of the ill-fated *Victoria*, leaving a hole of a hundred square yards in her hull.

Even in the face of such a terrible disaster, Sir George remained unperturbed. In the midst of the shouts of pain and confusion and desperate orders to save the day from further tragedy, the admiral seemed preoccupied with other matters not known to his fellow officers.

Tyron gave routine orders for the battleship to head for a nearby beach as if he were an automaton. The other ships under his command launched rescue boats toward the *Victoria* and the *Camperdown,* but the distracted admiral ordered them back. Only a few minutes before the doomed flagship began to sink did Sir George permit rescue efforts to begin.

There were shouts of fear and a mad scramble for the side—when the great battleship rolled on her side with a mighty shudder and sank. The rescue boats from the other ships in the fleet were helpless to aid the seamen being pulled down by the *Victoria,* for they had been ordered to return to their own vessels.

Three hundred and sixty men died in the sea tragedy. One of the fatalities was Admiral Sir George Tyron, who was last seen standing passively amidst the chaos, staring blankly about him as if in some kind of trance. His final command was to order away a midshipman who had approached him and expressed concern for his welfare.

The loss of the men and the flagship *Victoria* still ranks today as one of the strangest and most tragic losses in British naval history—especially tragic because it had been so unnecessary.

A court of inquiry was convened, but it was eventually dissolved when the baffled members were forced to conclude that the commander-in-chief of the Mediterranean Squadron, "as a result of a temporary aberration, made a most inexplicable and fatal mistake for which he paid with his life."

Back in the drawing rooms of London, however, there was much whispering over glasses of sherry about the bizarre phenomenon which had been witnessed by many of the most respectable and levelheaded men and women in all of England. Numerous influential individuals, many of them to be found in high places, swore to the fact that they had seen Sir George Tyron in his own drawing room at the same time that his lifeless body would have been floating in the waters of the Mediterranean—1,500 miles away.

• 35 •

While She Was Out of Her Body, She Brought Her Son Back from a Near-Death Experience

One of the most unusual cases in my files of near-death experiences involves a mother projecting out of her body, a dying son, and the spirit of a deceased friend. This account offers a dramatic demonstration that the essential self within us does survive physical death.

In 1972, times had grown very hard for the Levesque family of Aurora, Colorado. When Paul, the breadwinner of the large family, was almost fatally injured at work, his wife Nancy was left with the sole responsibility of providing for six children—all under the age of seventeen.

"Paul's employer was underinsured and we had had no insurance of our own," Nancy Levesque said. "What money we did receive didn't last long after all the medical bills had been deducted. Paul was left bedridden, and we didn't know at that time if he would ever be able to walk, to say nothing of being gainfully employed, ever again.

"I was a thirty-seven-year-old high school graduate with practically no work experience outside of the home," Nancy explained. "What kind of job could I get that would be able to bring us enough money to keep our heads above water financially?"

Michael, their seventeen-year-old son, picked up as many small part-time jobs as possible. "Michael wanted desperately to be able to help his dad and me support the family. He had always been a really conscientious boy, and when he saw that his part-time jobs just weren't helping all that much, he insisted on dropping out of high school in his senior year and looking for full-time employment."

Nancy and Paul would not listen to such a proposition. Somehow, they told Michael, the family would get by on the money that she was making as a part-time short-order cook and the dollars that he was bringing home with his several small jobs.

But then came the terrible day when they found the money and the note that Michael had left behind.

"He said that he could not stand being unable

to help us more," Nancy said. "Since he was the oldest, he wrote that he was going to strike out on his own and try to get a good job in a larger city. He would send every cent home that he could. In the meantime, he was leaving behind his special little nest egg of $35.10."

They were sick with worry. Michael was not a very tall boy, and he didn't weigh more than 135 pounds. He looked even younger than he was. He was naive and trusting—and he would probably be taken advantage of and exploited by too many unscrupulous employers. Or worse, he could easily be victimized by thugs on the road.

Nancy, Paul, and the children prayed each night during family devotions for the Lord to keep a safe watch over their Michael. The days passed into months, and no word arrived from their son. The worst part, Nancy said, was not knowing whether Michael was alive or dead.

"A thousand dreadful possibilities tormented me," she said. "I prayed to hear from him until it seemed as though my every breath became a prayer."

Incredibly, a year passed without word from their son.

And then, one night, eighteen months after Michael had left home, Nancy Levesque had her most unusual dream.

"It was just too real to have been an ordinary

dream. What it really was, we may not yet be able to understand."

According to Nancy's account, she was awakened in the dream by an insistent knocking at their back door. She got out of bed, fastened her bathrobe about her, and made her still-groggy way through to the kitchen.

She opened the door to find a young Chicano boy standing there, shivering with the cold.

Before she could say a word, her visitor spoke in urgent tones: "The boy is sick . . . come quick!"

Without thinking to question him further, Nancy motioned the boy, who was about the age of Michael, to come inside.

While he waited, she rushed to gather all of the spare sheets and bath towels in the house. All thought of sleep fled as she piled this linen collection into two huge bundles. She took one and handed the other to the boy.

They threw the bundles over their backs and walked out into the night. Nancy specifically remembers closing the door quietly behind her, so as not to awaken her husband and children, and then carefully closing the gate so the dog would not follow her.

Then, with the boy leading the way, they started to walk "quickly and with a gliding motion."

They hurried through the streets until they reached open country, then ". . . we fairly skimmed over the roads, uphill, downhill, so fast we seemed to fly."

They climbed mountains and crossed them "as if with wings"—then just as quickly, they descended.

"We crossed rivers as if we stood on tiny canoes that scooted us across the water without even getting our feet wet."

Nancy and her escort seemed to travel for hours—through mountains, open country, forests. Never once did they halt for drink or food, but kept moving relentlessly forward.

Nancy often found herself looking down on country that she had never seen before, but had read about in books and magazines.

"The trees were large," she recalled. "From the wide-spreading branches festoons of gray moss hung down like shimmering veils."

Then the road that they had been following wound up and down, over hummocks and through swamps. Finally, they came to a long, low building.

"The boy is here," the Chicano guide said.

And then they were inside, and the lad was leading her up a short, steep stairway, covered with dust and cobwebs.

They entered a windowless room, illumined only by the light from the cracks between the clapboard walls and the broken places in the roof. The place was heavy with a moldy, damp smell.

"Oh, Mom!" Nancy heard a familiar voice cry out faintly. "You've come!"

Her heart beating faster, Nancy rushed forward to discover her son Michael lying on a bare floor in a far corner of the attic. She fell to her knees, clutching her missing son to her breast, noting with alarm that his body was burning hot and that his face was dry and parched with fever.

"Oh, Mom," Michael moaned. "I'm so sick! I'm so sick with fever."

Nancy Levesque lost no time. She turned to the Chicano lad who had brought her there to ask him to bring buckets of cold water—and quickly.

She got busy gathering refuse from the floor which she wrapped into a pallet. Then she spread a cool, clean sheet over it.

Although Michael was a full-grown boy, she lifted him like a baby to settle him onto her hastily constructed bed.

By this time, Michael's friend had returned with the cold water. She dipped the towels and sheets one by one into the buckets of cool water, wrung them out lightly, then packed them around Michael's feverish body.

Hours later, she finally relaxed, knowing that the fever had broken. She could tell that the worst of her son's illness was over.

"Go to sleep, son," she said. "You'll get well now."

Without saying another word, Michael drifted immediately into a deep sleep.

Nancy sat quietly beside him, holding his hand, until she, too, slept.

She awoke in her own bed, tired and exhausted, every bone in her body aching.

Nancy was so weary that when she attempted to get out of bed, she found that she could not move. Again and again she made an effort to get out of bed, but she was too exhausted to lift her head from the pillow.

She called to Paul to tell him how completely enervated she was, and she told him about her strange dream.

"And don't tell me it was just a nightmare," she warned her husband. "Somehow, I know that I was really there with Michael. Paul, he's sick. I know it. Maybe he's dying. And he is somewhere a long, long way from here."

Paul told her to stay in bed and rest. The girls would help with breakfast and the other daily chores.

Nancy rolled over and slept the entire day, barely getting up in time to get to her job.

Two days later, the Levesques received a telegram from a county hospital in another state: "Come quickly. Your son frozen—possible amputation."

Nancy borrowed money from her sympathetic employer and boarded a bus for the journey to the little mountain town in Oregon where Michael was hospitalized. He suffered the amputation of a foot, but he recovered to full health.

One day, several weeks later, after Michael had returned to their home, Nancy decided to tell him about the strange dream that she had experienced.

Michael listened to the part about the Chicano boy who had knocked at the door, but when she began to describe the bizarre journey, he interrupted her.

"Let me give you some very important background information here, Mom," Michael said. "The boy's name is Alfredo Maqueda, but I called him José. You know, 'No way, José.' I know that somehow he saved my life. I guess, he's saved my life twice now."

Michael explained that he had been eating a sandwich in a fast-food restaurant when he glanced up to see a Mexican boy, about his own age, watching him through the window with such a hungry look on his face that Michael could not bear it. He motioned for the lad to come inside, and he ordered a sandwich for his companion.

Michael had left the restaurant and bade farewell to the Chicano, who was also wandering the country, looking for some kind of work.

Later that night, as he was walking past an alley in a rough part of town, two thugs jumped out of the darkness and blocked Michael's path.

They demanded whatever money he had, his coat, even the shoes that he was wearing.

Suddenly, the young Chicano pushed himself between Michael and the hoods. "No way," he insisted, brandishing a wicked-looking switchblade under their noses. "No way you gonna take this boy's money. No way! Now you get away, or I'll cut out your hearts!"

"Believe me," Michael told his mother, chuckling at the memory of Alfredo's fierce defense of him, "those punks hit the road."

Alfredo had smiled and told Michael: "No way I let them scum hurt you!"

Michael christened his newfound friend, "No Way, José," and the two of them teamed up together.

They picked up odd jobs here and there, always backing each other up. When the weather got colder, they decided to work their way south to a warmer climate.

The two teenage boys got as far south as Florida and were living there when one of the devasting hurricanes that periodically rip into the coastal regions hit that southern state.

Michael and Alfredo had been camping on the beach when a hurricane caught them unexpectedly. A huge wave had reared up and crashed down on them, sweeping them off their feet. Another angry wave hit them, and they were now at the mercy of the storm.

"Somehow, José got hold of me and managed

to pull me onto the beach," Michael said, tears welling in his eyes. "I don't know how he did it, but he got me to a place where I was able to get a good hold on a branch or something.

"Just as I turned to see how José was making it, another wave swept him out to sea. I never saw him again. He had saved me . . . then lost his own life."

Michael began to work his way back toward Colorado and his parents' home, but when someone offered him a job at a forestry camp in Oregon, the money seemed too good to pass up. Maybe now, for the first time, he would be able to save enough to send home to be of help to the family's financial burdens.

Then he had come down with the illness and the terrible fever. He tried to keep working, but one day he had collapsed and had spent the night in the forest, exposed to freezing temperatures. The next morning when his foreman had found him, he had rushed him to the county hospital.

Michael spent most of the time in an unconscious or semiconscious state. Occasionally, he did come to, at least enough to realize that he was in a hospital—and that he was so ill he might lose his life.

In his fevered mind, Michael believed himself to be shut up in some musty, dirty old attic, covered with cobwebs and crawling with spiders.

His body felt most of the time like a furnace of hot coals. "But I did not want to die. And, like a frightened little boy, I wanted my mother!

"Oh, Mom, whenever I could think at all, I wanted you. And I prayed—or tried to pray— that you would come . . . that somehow God would send you to me so that you would take care of me."

Michael knew that he had left his physical body on numerous occasions. "I could see my body below me, and I knew that I was dying."

Then one night he had awakened to find No-Way-José standing at his bedside. "Amigo, it does not go so well for you. What can I do to help you?"

Michael asked his friend to go bring his mother to him. "Please, José. Please. As fast as you can!"

Michael fell into a semiconscious state and found himself back in that detestable attic place. He was lying on the bare floor, surrounded by refuse and debris. The place was damp and smelly—and he knew that he was sicker than ever before.

And then before his painfully burning eyes, he saw José come into the attic with his mother.

Michael was able to recount to his mother all that she had done that night to save him and how José had worked to help her. Finally, he had heard his mother tell him to sleep, and he had drifted into the sweet oblivion of a healing slumber.

He had awakened in the hospital where a nurse stood taking his pulse. And he was at last rational enough to give her his parents' address in Colorado.

Nancy and her son compared the dates of their two extraordinary experiences and they found them to be the same. The night that she had had her bizarre "dream" had been the night that Michael had passed the critical stage of his illness. He had awakened that morning with a normal temperature, thus encouraging the medical personnel to proceed with the required surgery.

"Michael has always insisted that someway or somehow, I had actually been there with him that night he was so near death," Nancy concluded her account. "And I wholeheartedly agree. Someway or somehow, his friend José—Alfredo Maqueda—had come from Beyond to bring me to my son's side."

• 36 •

During a High Fever, She Lived Two Days in One

In 1981, Mrs. Patricia Fellar worked as a cook in a restaurant in Tempe, Arizona, while her husband Louis was completing his work on his doctorate at the university.

Her daily schedule was a busy one, requiring her to rise every morning at five-thirty if she wanted any breakfast for herself before she began cooking for everyone else, including Louis and the kids, seven-year-old Lisa and ten-year-old Tammy. Louis also worked part-time at a filling station, so he needed a solid breakfast before he went in at seven, and Patricia had always believed in the kids having a nutritious breakfast to fill them with positive energy for school.

During the heavy tourist season during the winter months, Patricia's work load seemed to increase to such a degree that it appeared as though the days would stretch into weeks. During this period, she would be so exhausted when she came home that all she felt like doing was falling into a deep, weary sleep.

And after a month or two of the increased work load, the combination of cooking at the restaurant and caring for two small children soon conspired against housework. Patricia, normally a very conscientious housekeeper, would wince when she saw the laundry piling up, the dust gathering, the floors of their rented apartment growing in grime.

She knew that Louis was trying to help out in the spic and span department, but he spent all afternoon in classes, his evenings studying, and his mornings working at the gas station.

"Dear God," she began praying aloud, "if only I could afford a day off to catch up with the housework and get the extra rest that I can feel my body is beginning to demand."

On a Thursday, one night in February, Patricia came home with a fever. She knew it was the darn bug that was going around. Nearly everyone at work had been out with it. But she couldn't afford to take any sick time.

She took her temperature and saw that it was 103.4 degrees. Not at all good for a woman to be running such a high fever. She took a couple of aspirins and went to bed without mentioning anything to Louis.

Patricia could not recall when she had ever felt so bone tired.

"Even before I set my alarm clock, I felt as though my conscious self was slipping out of my body. I figured that I must really be sick and starting to hallucinate, because I felt as if the 'real me' was standing apart from my physical body, just kind of checking things out."

Because she felt so tired and so "weird," Patricia was extremely concerned about her being able to get up in time in the morning. Before turning out the light, she checked and rechecked her alarm clock to be certain that it would go off at the right time.

On Friday morning she awoke and looked at her clock.

She sat bolt upright when she read *seven-thirty*.

She was two hours late.

The alarm had not gone off!

As her mind spun with possible explanations, the only one that made sense was that Louis had felt her fever during the night, assessed how ill she was, and had decided to shut off her alarm and let her sleep.

And—bless his heart—he had also got Lisa and Tammy up and quietly got them off to school.

As she slowly got dressed, feeling really quite

good and wondering what her next course of action should be, Patricia all at once decided that this must be the day off for which she had been praying so earnestly to God. This must be the day that she was supposed to catch up on her housework—and if that meant losing her job, then so be it. Another of the restaurants in the Arizona college town had already approached her about coming to work in their kitchen, so if her boss didn't like her taking a day off once in a blue moon, then it was meant to be. And knowing her husband's thoroughness, she just knew that he had already called in sick for her.

First she went to work on the bathroom, scrubbing all the fixtures until they were bright and shiny.

Next she launched a full-scale attack on the kitchen with its dishes, cupboards, and floors—all to be cleaned.

Finally, she attacked the small dining room, where a large basket of ironing awaited her.

All in all, Patricia Fellar dusted, scrubbed, waxed, washed, folded, and ironed until she could say with full satisfaction that her house was clean. Slick as a whistle!

And then the alarm went off.

With an abrupt sense of confusion, Patricia reached for the clock. *It was five-thirty!*

She sat up and saw Louis pull the covers

over his head to catch a few minutes more of snoozing time.

She looked in on her children and saw that they were still sleeping.

Patricia shook Tammy awake and asked her what day it was.

Tammy's eyelids fluttered into wakefulness, and she stretched and yawned before she answered with a giggle. "Mommy, it's Friday. You always know what day it is! You're teasing me!"

Patricia Fellar did not know what day this *day* was. How could it be Friday, when yesterday— Friday—was her stay-at-home cleaning day? Today had to be Saturday!

Louis was up, heading for the bathroom for his morning shower. "You feeling better, honey?" he asked. "I could tell that you had a pretty high fever during the night."

Patricia nodded. She felt better. Then she had to ask: "What day is it today, Lou?"

"It's TGIF, babe. Thank God It's Friday. Why, did you lose a day?"

Patricia looked around the house in stunned amazement. Everywhere she saw the obvious results of her labors—clean floors, ironed and folded clothes, polished fixtures.

She hadn't *lost* a day. Rather, she had *gained* one!

When she thought back, it suddenly occurred to her that in a very real sense, time had not seemed to exist. She had worked an entire "day" without having seen Louis, the girls—or without having fed them . . . or herself, for that matter. She had worked like a madwoman without food or drink or rest. And her fever had completely disappeared.

Somehow, Patricia Fellar stated in her fascinating account, she had managed to live two days in one.

"I have always been intrigued by the true nature of time," she wrote. "Is it truly a dimension unto itself? Or maybe I had entered another aspect of physical time when that terrible fever projected me out-of-the body and into another dimension of reality? I have lots of questions that I would like someone to answer, but the proof lay in the physical evidence of the tangible results of my nonexistent day's work!"

• 37 •

An Atheist Is Amazed to Find Himself Knocking at Heaven's Door

Dr. Robert Crookall reports a case first published in the *Moscow Journal* in 1916. The subject of the near-death experience was a Russian who had rejected any concept of survival after physical death.

The subject remembered feeling dizzy during a stay in the hospital. He called for a doctor, then, strangely, became aware of a "certain state of division" within himself. He was conscious, and yet, at the same time, he was experiencing a growing feeling of indifference toward his physical well-being. It even seemed as if he was losing the capacity for registering physical sensations.

"It seemed as if two beings were manifesting within me," he said. "One—the main part of me—was concealed deep within. The other, my physical body, external and less significant."

He began to feel the "main part" of himself being drawn somewhere with irresistible force. He felt as though he were being brought back to a place that was now reclaiming that which he had been allowed to use on Earth for a brief period of time. At the same time, he was filled with the conviction that his essential self, the "main part" of him, would not disappear.

He was dimly aware that it seemed as if the entire medical staff of the hospital was crowded around his bed, each of them striving to improve his condition.

Then the "main part" of himself moved forward and upward, and he saw his physical husk lying there below him on the hospital bed.

He tried to grasp the hand of his physical body, but his spirit hand went through it.

"Struck by this strange phenomenon," he said, "I wanted someone to help me understand what was happening."

He called to the principal physician, but the air did not seem to transmit the sound waves of his voice.

He tried in every manner which he could conceive to make his presence known, but none of the medical staff seemed to be at all aware of his Real Self.

Had he died?

He found the question inconceivable, for

death meant the cessation of life—and he had not lost consciousness for even a single moment.

He was as aware of himself as ever. He could see, hear, move, touch, and think.

Even when he heard the doctor declare to other members of the medical staff that it was "all over," the perplexed Russian refused to accept the idea of his death.

A nurse turned to a religious icon and asked for peace on his soul.

The words had scarcely been uttered when two angels manifested at his side.

"They picked me up by my arms and carried me right through the wall and into the street. Then we began to ascend quickly."

As he ascended with the two angelic guardians, he noticed certain remarkable features of existence in his spirit body. Although it was dark, he was able to see everything clearly. And he was able to perceive a much greater expanse than he would have with his ordinary vision.

As the ascent continued, they were suddenly surrounded by a "throng of hideous beings, evil spirits," which tried to snatch him away from the angel guides.

In what must have been a remarkable experience for the atheist, he found himself praying for deliverance from the negative entities. To the nonbeliever's astonishment, as if in answer to his prayer, there appeared a "white mist which concealed them from the ugly spirits."

Their ascent upward was halted when an intense light appeared before them, and a mighty voice thundered, "Not ready!" At once, the angels began to descend with him.

"I did not understand the real sense of the words, but soon the outlines of a city became visible. I saw the hospital . . . I was carried into a room completely unknown to me. In this room there stood a row of tables, and on one of them, covered over with a sheet, I saw my dead body.

"One of my guardian angels pointed to my body and said 'Enter.' "

The Russian felt at first as though something were pressing close about him.

There was a sensation of unpleasant cold.

A sensation of ever-increasing tightness continued, and just before he lost consciousness, he felt very sad, "as though [he] had lost something."

When he next became aware of his surroundings, he was once again in the hospital ward. The head physician sat at his bedside, astounded by the medical miracle which the entire staff had just witnessed.

They failed to understand the importance of what had occurred to their patient, but in his own mind, "There is no doubt in the veracity of that which I have written—my soul temporarily left my body and thereafter returned to it."

• 38 •

Native American Shamanism and the Near-Death Experience

In 1865, the great warrior Roman Nose, under the tutelage of White Bull, an elderly Cheyenne medicine man, lay on a raft for four days in the midst of a sacred lake. Roman Nose was in a trance so deep that he would have appeared dead to any other than the initiated. He partook of no food, no water; and he suffered a relentless sun by day and pouring rain by night.

When he returned from the "land of the grandfathers," the place of spirits, Roman Nose had obtained the necessary vision teachings to attack the Blue Coats who were invading the Powder River.

On the day of battle, Roman Nose mounted his white pony and told the assembled warriors not to accompany his charge until the white soldiers had emptied their rifles at him. The power that he had received during his "little death" had rendered him impervious to the Blue Coats' bullets.

Roman Nose broke away from the war party and urged his pony into a run toward the ranks of white soldiers standing before their wagons. When he was so near that he could see their faces, Roman Nose wheeled his mount and rode parallel to their ranks and their rifles.

He had made three or four passes before volley after volley from the soldiers' Springfield muskets. He remained unhit, unscratched. Finally, a musket ball smashed his pony out from under him, but Roman Nose rose untouched and signaled his warriors to attack the Blue Coats. The magic that he had received during his self-created near-death experience would keep him safe from the white man's bullets.

The respected medicine practitioner, Black Elk of the Oglala Sioux, received a powerful vision during a near-death experience that made him a "hole," a port of entry for the spirits to enter the physical world.

Rather than the term, "hole," today's metaphysical practitioner might say that he or she was a "medium" or a "channel" through which the power from the spirit world might flow. And just as Black Elk never failed to credit the "outer world" for his ability to focus the healing or clairvoyant energies, so do the more conscientious of our contemporary mystics always appear conscious of the true source of their abilities. It appears that it may be a universal spiritual law that those who are chosen to serve as "holes" for higher plane intelligences must be ever-mindful of their being but stewards for their unique talents.

In 1890, Jack Wilson, a powerfully built, darkly handsome Paiute who worked as a ranch hand for a white rancher, came down with a terrible fever. His sickness became so bad that for three days he lay as if dead.

When he returned to consciousness and to the arms of his wife Mary, he told the Paiutes who had assembled around his "dead" body that his spirit had walked with God, the Old Man, for those three days; and the Old Man had given him a powerful vision to share with the Paiute people.

Jack Wilson's grandfather had been the esteemed prophet Wodziwob. His father had been the respected holy man Tavibo. Among his own people, Jack Wilson was known as Wovoka; and now he, too, had spent his time of initiation in death and had emerged as a holy man and a prophet.

Wovoka's vision proclaimed that the dead of many tribes were all alive, waiting to be reborn.

If the native peoples wished the buffalo to return, the grasses to grow tall, the rivers to run clean, they must not injure anyone; they must not do harm to any living thing. They must not make war. They must lead lives of purity, cease gambling, put away strong drink, and guard themselves against all lusts of the flesh.

The most important part of the vision that God gave to Wovoka was the Ghost Dance. The Paiute prophet told his people that the dance had never been performed anywhere on Earth. It was the dance of the spirit people of the Other World. To perform this dance was to insure that God's blessings would be bestowed upon the tribe.

Wovoka said that the Old Man had spoken to him as if he were his son. He assured him that many miracles would be worked through him. The native people had received their messiah.

I feel that I must briefly point out yet another aspect of the NDE phenomenon for purposes of cultural comparison and contrast and to better serve the Oneness of our common spirituality.

While our contemporary society is currently in the process of rediscovering the near-death experience, other societies and psycho-spiritual systems have never lost its power and its truth— and its practical applications in their mundane existences.

Whereas we still speak of the experience reluctantly and applaud the courage of those who dare to share their accounts of the spiritual strength, courage, and hope that it has brought to their lives, for the Native American shaman, as we may see from these few brief examples, the near-death experience was almost a requirement to become an accomplished medicine practitioner. In other societies as well, it appears nearly a precondition that those who aspire for the position of shaman have at some time undergone an illness, an accident, a terrible fever wherein they appeared to have died.

The anthropologist Ivar Lissner defines a shaman as one ". . . who knows how to deal with spirits and influence them . . . The essential characteristic of the shaman is his excitement, his ecstasy and trancelike condition. . . . [The elements which constitute this ecstasy are] a form of self-severance from mundane existence, a state of heightened sensibility and spiritual awareness. The shaman loses outward consciousness and becomes inspired or enraptured. While in this state of enthusiasm, he sees dreamlike apparitions, hears voices, and receives visions of truth. More than that, his soul sometimes leaves his body to go wandering."

What we are only now beginning to treat once again with respect and awe—the out-of-body and near-death experience—the shaman, the medicine practitioner, has understood for centuries. These sincere priests of their people believe that, from time to time, the essential self, the soul, leaves the physical shell of the body to travel to other dimensions of existence for the purpose of receiving spiritual insights which are not possible even in deep meditation.

The aforementioned Black Elk was only a boy of nine when he heard voices telling him "it was time" to receive his first great vision.

Black Elk fell terribly ill and was taken out of his body by two spirit guides who told him that they were to take him to the land of his grandfathers. Here, in the land of the spirits, Black Elk received the great vision that was to sustain him all of his life.

When he was returned to his body, his parents greeted the first fluttering of his eyelids with great joy. Black Elk had been lying as if dead for twelve days.

In whatever manner the reader of these chronicles of the near-death experience chooses to assess the material in this book, there should be little question remaining that thousands of men and women have been elevated to higher realms of consciousness and spiritual communion. They have made contact with a source of power and inspiration beyond the ordinary, and they enjoy increased creativity, peace of mind, and joy.

Perhaps, in one sense, they, too, have become very much like shamans in their own families and communities. They have discovered to their eternal satisfaction that there is a nonphysical self—a soul—that exists within them. What is more, they have learned that this soul is capable of being activated as an inner source of inestimable power that, in turn, is linked to an even greater Source of power and inspiration that permeates and governs the entire universe. They have acquired all this knowledge—because they have become One with the Light.

• 39 •

She Received a Preview of Heaven Before Her Final Transition

In 1973, a retired clergyman provided me with the following inspirational account of one his parishioners who received a comforting preview of Heaven during a near-death experience.

Mrs. Millie Dorrance lay dying and felt her spirit leaving her body. As her consciousness seemed to bob somewhere between the physical and nonphysical dimensions, she saw a brilliant light descending toward her.

She was drawn to the light, and as her spirit body came nearer to the brilliant illumination, she perceived that the bright light was actually the aura of radiance around an angel. Later, Mrs. Dorrance told her pastor, family, and friends that the angel was lovelier than any language could ever describe.

The angelic being carried a cross in one hand and a wandlike instrument in the other.

The angel touched Millie with the wand, and the woman felt a flame of holy love spread throughout her entire spirit body.

"The cross," the angel explained to her, "is the symbol of sacrificial love—without which there is no Heaven."

After a brief dialogue concerning the true nature of Divine Love, the angel escorted Millie to a heavenly abode.

"I saw another beautiful angel instructing the souls of children who had died young about the earthly life of Jesus," Millie said. "These poor little ones had died before they had received any proper kind of religious instruction.

"Their lessons were given in what might be called 'spiritual moving pictures.' The story of Jesus was presented much like it is in the Bible, but it was told more from the angelic, or heavenly, point of view."

Millie Dorrance went on to explain that she was permitted to watch the 'spiritual moving pictures' long enough to view a depiction of Jesus before his resurrection, walking among the tombs and speaking to the dead who he had redeemed.

"I saw the picture-teachings of Jesus reentering his body. I heard God's voice say, 'This is my beloved son, the bright morning star. Peace to the world.' "

After a few more inspirational sessions of instruction, Millie was told by the beautiful angel that she must return to Earth to share her experiences with others.

"I was extremely disappointed to learn that I was not yet ready to stay in the higher world," she said, "but I was informed that it was not yet time for my 'graduation.' "

To give her spiritual strength to endure the continued separation from Heaven and to perform her ministry on Earth, Millie was given a golden goblet from which she drank a marvelous liquid that seemed to be composed of light and love.

Millie Dorrance was also given a definite period of time during which she would stay on Earth.

"I know the hour of my passing," she told those closest to her, "and when it comes, I have been promised a glorious return to Heaven."

The beautiful angel of Light, who had been her heavenly guide, escorted Millie back to Earth so that she might reenter her physical body and begin her true mission among her fellow humans.

The retired clergyman who gave me the account of Millie Dorrance testified that the woman served as an inspiration to all who knew her during the remaining days of her life.

"And she never once wavered in her account of her marvelous sojourn in Heaven," he told me.

The clergyman was at her bedside with her family when Millie lay dying for the "second time." She had confided in her beloved ones that her appointed day and hour had arrived.

"I will praise my Heavenly Father, for my hope in Jesus is worth more to me than ten thousand worlds," the inspired woman said reverently.

"Then, being fully apprised of her allotted time," the clergyman concluded, "Mrs. Dorrance sang a favorite hymn and completed her final transition to the higher world."

• 40 •

God Is Light!

Mrs. Jo Peters of Honolulu, Hawaii, told me of a most interesting experience which her little three-year-old daughter Andrea had in December 1971.

"In a matter of fifteen minutes, Andrea came down with a fever of 106 degrees!

"I quickly started putting her in ice packs and gave her vitamin C. During the evening her fever would get down to 104, then it would go back up to 106."

Jo kept a watchful eye on her daughter all through the night. Her background is in nursing, psychology, and nutrition. She told me that although she had passed her state board exams in

Hawaii, she had decided not to go into formal practice.

Because of her awareness of various healing techniques, Jo continued to keep Andrea in cold water throughout the long hours of darkness, and the next morning the child's fever was nearly gone.

At eleven-thirty that morning, Jo was holding Andrea in her arms, relieved that her fever had broken.

"Andrea was lying across my lap—and all of a sudden she began to laugh. Then she made a horrible face and breathed in forcefully.

"Several times I asked her what was wrong, but she didn't answer me."

Jo was becoming anxious. Andrea was staring up at the ceiling, and she began to describe a scene that she was somehow perceiving.

"I asked her to tell me about it. She said that it was made up of the most beautiful colors.

"I was puzzled by this, because Andrea does not do well with colors. She's four now, and she still gets them mixed up.

"She said she saw the color blue. She described some other colors—then she screamed horribly!

"After this terrible scream, she began to smile again. 'I see Jesus on the cross,' she said."

Jo stressed the point that her family was not Roman Catholic. Their children know about Jesus, but they had never taught them about Jesus on the cross.

"He is looking at the little animals and talking to them," Andrea said.

Then she told her mother: "The Light is sooo beautiful! It is gold and yellow."

Andrea startled Jo with another scream, then she smiled, just as she had done before, and said, "I see God. Oh, Mommy—God is Light! *God is Light*!"

Jo told me that she had never taught Andrea such a thing. "I have always said that God is Love. But she kept repeating over and over that God is Light and that He is so beautiful. Andrea is not a dramatic child, and she never talks expressively."

But then all of a sudden, Andrea clutched her mother and cried out, "No, no, Mommy! I don't want to go there yet! I don't want to go into the Light yet! Please keep it away from me!"

"Andrea hugged me very tight, then came out of it," Jo said. "It was ended. I knew then that her sickness had passed.

"I talked to Andrea later, and she remembered the experience clearly—but each day it seemed to fade a bit in her memory. Now when I talk about it, she doesn't know to what I am referring.

"But when I look back on the experience, I am certain that we nearly lost Andrea. I think she came close to passing on."

Jo Peters told me that she was very thankful that the Light wasn't yet ready to claim her little daughter.

· 41 ·

Remaining at One with the Light

Deon Frey of Chicago had survived a near-death experience in which her Soul Body had become One with the Light. Then, during meditation sometime later, she found that she had managed to summon the heavenly light while she was on the Earth plane and very much in her physical body.

"I remember being in meditation for quite some time and sitting in my room this night when all of a sudden the whole room was filled with light, as if the sun were shining brightly," she said.

"The light seemed to be emanating from one corner of the room, and it seemed as though I could almost make out a form.

"The color of the light was indescribable. It had edges of violet hue, but it was crystal white—or mother of pearl—and so bright that it almost blinded me.

"Once again, I had a feeling of Oneness with it, a unity. It was like being one with everything all at once. It was like a feeling of love that one really can't understand on the Earth plane, because it's such a spiritual envelopment. You want to stay. You don't want to return. You don't want to come back to physical consciousness—although you are in a conscious awareness.

"Although I heard no voice, I was filled with a knowing quality. I just *knew* things. It wasn't as if the light were speaking to me, but it seemed to give me direct answers to a lot of questions on my mind.

"For a moment I thought that the light was going to form into the Ancient of Ancients. I seemed to have an awareness that the light could be male, it could be female—or it could be both. But I knew whatever it was, it was not anything that I should ever fear.

"I think this is what is meant by becoming One with the Light and letting your light shine forth," Deon concluded.

Al G. Manning, a 1950 Magna Cum Laude graduate from UCLA with a degree in business administration, who has served in an executive capacity at two aerospace manufacturing and research firms, became One with the Light during an out-of-body experience many years ago.

"I was in the middle of this shaft of light," he recalled. "I could feel the warmth and the love."

Al told me that even though a voice had spoken to him from the stream of light, he was not allowed to bring back any messages from the experience.

Later, however, he learned how to practice a sacred worship ceremony by touching the Light and feeling the response of love.

"I sit down at my private altar each morning and evening," he said. "The first thing that I do is to reach up to my highest concept of God, to something far greater than I, and I *expect* a response.

"No, I do not *always* find the room brightened and find myself bathed in light, but there is always a response. There is a *feeling*—and it is not just subjective, either.

"But every time I reach for the Light—whether I am at a big business conference or sitting comfortably before my altar or driving down the street—I expect a response. If I don't get one, I stop everything until I do, because to be that far out of tune would just be chaos to me.

"Before I leave my altar, I reattune myself with the Light and send it before me. The affirmation I use varies somewhat, but basically, it is this:

" 'Now I direct the Light to go before me to make the path easy and the way straight.

" 'May the Light bring upliftment, inspiration, effectiveness, enthusiasm, and joy to everyone who comes close to my aura.

" 'I am Light going to meet Light—and only goodness can result.' "

Lasca Schroeppel of Chicago has encountered the Light during her own out-of-body traveling, and she said that she has sometimes theorized that her Soul Body may serve as a kind of prism that breaks up the heavenly Light for better spiritual utilization.

"Sometimes instead of seeing a blinding light, I will see the complete spectrum of the rainbow," she explained, "and I feel that the perhaps the 'prism' is my Soul Body that takes the spiritual energy which is always there and breaks it up for my use and comprehension.

"When I see this white light, it is not like an ordinary light source. It is frequently accompanied by a very clear, pure tone without harmonics.

"This light is so inconceivably brilliant that it is almost as if it is being drilled into me with many little protons of light—each with individual energy, yet collectively pure and bright.

"I feel that when you are able to become a vehicle for this Light that you have offered yourself—or identified yourself—with the Divine," she said. "Sometimes I feel that I have pure energy going through my hands."

Almost without exception, those who have become One with the Light during a near-death or out-of-body experience have stated that their sense of time was obscured; and while they were in this state of the Eternal Now, they realized a sense of unity with all things.

In my conversations with Al G. Manning, he commented that, in his opinion, his feeling of the Light was comparable to the kind of illumination experience expressed by the Hindu in *samadhi* or the *satori* of the Zen Buddhist or the Holy Spirit of Christianity.

In her autobiographical *Don't Fall Off the Mountain*, Shirley MacLaine writes of the night that she lay shivering in a Bhutanese house in the Paro Valley of the Himalayas. Her teeth chattered, and her insides "tied themselves in knots."

As she lay wondering how she might overcome the terrible cold, she remembered the words of a Yoga instructor in Calcutta who had told her that there was a center in her mind that was her "nucleus, the center of your universe." Once she had found this nucleus, he had said, pain, fear, sorrow—nothing could touch her.

"It will look like a tiny sun," he had instructed her. "The sun is the center of every solar system and the reason for all life on all planets in all universes. So it is with yours."

Shirley closed her eyes, searched for the center of her mind.

Then the room "left" her. The cold room and the wind outside began to leave her conscious mind.

"Slowly in the center of my mind's eye a tiny round ball appeared," she writes. "I stared and stared at it. Then I felt I became the orange ball."

The center of her own private universe began to grow and to generate heat. The heat spread down through her neck and arms and finally stopped in her stomach. She felt drops of perspiration on her midriff and forehead.

The light continued to grow brighter and brighter until she sat up on the cot with a start and opened her eyes, fully expecting to find that someone had turned on a light.

Dripping with perspiration, she was stunned to find the room dark.

As she lay back, she felt as though she were glowing. Still perspiring, she fell asleep.

Her instructor had been correct. Hidden within herself there was something much greater than her outer self.

Once when I was discussing such matters as near-death experiences, out-of-body projections, and becoming One with the Light with the great psychic-sensitive Harold Sherman, he commented that there apparently existed a "higher-most level of consciousness" which we very seldom touched, except, perhaps, in such experiences as the near-death journey that brought us in our Soul Bodies to the heavenly dimensions.

"We can't even comprehend in what form the God-conscious Mind exists," he said, "but we can feel its presence; we can express it in terms of light."

Reflecting that when one has been surrounded by the radiance of the Light he or she is often given an awareness of some particular spiritual truth, Sherman expressed his opinion that we probably couldn't make too much of a conscious effort to achieve such a state of Oneness. "Trying too hard might short-circuit the experience," he said. "If you try too hard, you activate your imagination and then you self-hallucinate."

I granted Harold that he had made a very important point.

Continuing his observations, he said that such experiences were not rewarded according to any kind of scale of "deservability to determine our meriting of that kind of experience.

"It is a condition that exists," he said, "and when our own mental attitudes or emotional natures happen to be right, we hit a higher frequency for a moment—and all of a sudden something happens.

"Through an application of meditation and concentration to determine our relationship to the

God-consciousness within, we can prove to our-selves that these powers do exist and that they work.

"We should all work on cleansing our minds, getting rid of the hates and the resentments and the fears in our consciousness and strive to make ourselves clear and true channels for contact with the Cosmic Conscious level of the mind."

· 42 ·

Reflecting the Heavenly Light with Meditation

In 1973, I received a letter from Dr. Carolyn M. of Florida, who told me that she had encountered the light of cosmic consciousness, which, she believed, enabled her to meet the heavenly light after her brother made his transition to the other side.

When she had come into cosmic consciousness, she wrote, the brilliant light that came to her seemed to burn her eyelids and fill her body. "It has been a constant inspiration to me, and in deep meditation, I still get that indescribable light."

In addition to maintaining her contact with the Light, Dr. M. said that she traveled with her brother to his dimension in the afterlife.

Although her brother passed from physical life many years before, he has come three time to lift her out of her body while she is sleeping.

"He puts his arms around me, and we float out into space. The last time he came, I saw my body lying on the bed—and then we were out in open space. For weeks after these experiences, I seem to be lifted up in consciousness—and oh, so very happy!"

Psychic-sensitive Betty Allen told me that one night, while she sat working at her typewriter, she was suddenly bathed in a golden light.

"It was just like being flooded with love," she said, "and I felt as though I were sitting in a beam of light. I realized then that there was a remarkable world beyond my ordinary senses. I realized that I was a part of it, and I knew that I wasn't really struggling alone."

In 1985, my wife, Sherry Hansen Steiger, who has practiced meditation for many years and who appears able to go very deeply into altered states of consciousness, was able to travel in another dimension and visit what she believed may have been the New Jerusalem. Sherry had undergone near-death experiences on two prior occasions: once as a child suffering from rheumatic fever and again as an adult when she ran a near-fatal fever during a kidney infection.

Sherry, who comes from a very fundamentalist

religious family and who is herself an ordained Protestant minister, has found great strength and guidance from her times of deep meditation. On this particular occasion, she remained in an extremely intense meditative state for nearly five hours.

After praying and relaxing, she remembered leaving her body in a sudden "poof."

As she left for "somewhere," she was met by a Light Being, who would serve as her escort through "the most mystically beautiful experience of my life."

In her own words:

"As audacious as this may sound, I truly felt as though in some way I saw or touched the Divine Force. The Light Being, a facet of the Divine Force, was so loving and caring and showed me so many things. The Being did not seem to have a gender, but I felt as though I knew him/her.

"It seemed as though we traveled through galaxies, making stops along the way.

"There was one place—maybe it was a planet . . . maybe it was the New Jerusalem—where the beauty was far above anything I've ever dreamed possible. It was like a crystal/diamond planet, reflecting and refracting the purest, most brilliant colors. The light all around was effervescent.

"As a 'living crystal' I became fused with the light.

"I *became* the Light!

"Blissful elation permeated every cell of my beingness. How I wished that others might be able to experience this powerful love . . . this perfect love.

"Not long after that—or so it seemed—the Light Being told me that I had to go back. I was told that I would only remember a small part of what I had seen. More would be revealed to my conscious mind as I shared and used the experience to help others.

"For three subsequent days, I felt a little 'spacey' after the experience. Additional glimpses of the vision have gradually come back to me.

"I *know* there is an absolute reality . . . a life beyond . . . a continuation of life . . . a perfect, all-encompassing power of love and peace, order and law.

"This absolute reality is the love we are to be . . . it's the love we were . . . it's the love we are."

To engage in a metaphysical debate whether the light received in meditation or the cosmic consciousness experience can compare or equal the light encountered during the near-death experience would seem largely futile and certainly beyond the province of this present book.

In my opinion, it seems apparent that throughout the centuries of humankind's spiritual questing and seeking, those individuals who have experienced both the Oneness with the Light through the near-death experience and the Oneness with the Light through illumination or cosmic consciousness have felt that a sincere and disciplined program of meditation might somehow at least reflect the power and majesty of the Heavenly Light and be able to summon at least a portion of Divine Love into their earthly existence.

Numerous mystics and disciplined meditators have spoken of the brilliant light that surrounded them during the onset of a vision, a revelation, or an illumination experience. And almost without exception, those who have experienced the sudden flooding light have stated that their sense of time was obscured and that while in such a state of the Eternal Now, they realized a sense of unity and oneness with all things.

In his chapter on "Basic Mystical Experience" in his superb *Watcher on the Hills,* Dr. Raynor C. Johnson, Master of Queen's College, University of Melbourne, lists seven characteristics of illumination:

1. *The appearance of light*: "This observation is uniformly made, and may be regarded as a criterion of the contact of soul and spirit."
2. *Ecstasy, love, bliss*: "Almost all the accounts refer to the supreme emotional tones of the experience."

3. *The approach to One-ness*: "In the union of soul with Spirit, [one] acquires a sense of unity with all things."

4. *Insights given to numerous subjects.*

5. *Positive effect on health and vitality.*

6. *Sense of time obscured.*

7. *Effects on living*: Dr. Johnson quotes a recipient of the illumination experience: "It's significance for me has been incalculable and has helped me through sorrows and stresses which, I feel, would have caused shipwreck in my life without the clearly remembered refreshment and undying certainty of this one experience."

Surely, it is clear after even a cursory examination of Dr. Johnson's seven characteristics of illumination that each one of them may also be applied to the near-death experience. And while no one can state with complete assurance and authority that one experience may equal the other, I feel confident in affirming that a disciplined program of meditation might surely be able to approximate and "reflect" the extraordinary sense of Oneness which is achieved when one blends with the Light during the near-death experience.

In his *An Introduction to Zen Buddhism*, D. T. Suzuki quotes Professor Nukairya's description of *satori*, the state of illumination attained by reaching a higher level of consciousness:

"It is the godly light, the inner heaven, the key to all the treasures of the mind, the focal point of thought and consciousness, the source of power and might, the seat of goodness, of justice, of sympathy, of the measure of all things. When this inmost knowledge is fully awakened, we are able to understand that each of us is identical in spirit, in being and in nature with universal life, or Buddha, etc."

In his *Varieties of Religious Experience*, William James quotes Vivekananda's work on Raja Yoga, which was published in London in 1896, in regard to the state of mystical insight known as *samadhi*:

"The mind itself has a higher state of existence, beyond reason, a superconscious state, and . . . when the mind gets to that higher state, then this knowledge beyond reasoning comes. . . .

"Just as unconscious work is beneath consciousness, so there is another work which is above consciousness, and which, also, is not accompanied with the feeling of egoism. . . . There is no feeling of *I*, and yet the mind works, desireless, free from restlessness, objectless, bodiless.

"Then the Truth shines in its full effulgence, and we know ourselves—for *Samadhi* lies potential in us all—for what we truly are, free, immortal, omnipotent, loosed from the finite, and its contrasts of good and evil altogether, and identical with the Atman or Universal Soul."

The Hindu scripture *Bhagavad-Gita*'s instruction on how best to practice Yoga ends with the promise that ". . . when the mind of the Yogi is in harmony and finds rest in the Spirit within, all restless desires gone, then he is a *Yukta,* one in God. Then his soul is a lamp whose light is steady, for it burns in a shelter where no winds come."

Guided Visualizations to Assist You in Reflecting the Heavenly Light in Your Own Life

At various awareness seminars which I have conducted around the United States during the past twenty-five years, I have served as a guide who leads groups of students through a number of inner journeys, including meeting the Golden Light, their angelic guide, and viewing the Heavenly Kingdom. The goal of these sessions is solely that of raising individual awareness and permitting people to gain a clearer picture of what their true mission on Earth may be. This information is presented in a totally undogmatic manner. No creeds or philosophies are expounded at the expense of any other.

I have assembled the techniques which I now

share with you from bits and pieces of my own near-death experience, my own meditations, and the insights which I have gained from over forty years of study in the spiritual and metaphysical fields. I make no claims of illumination or of special knowledge that you may receive from employing these techniques in your own inner explorations, but I offer them to you in a spirit of love and goodwill.

You may wish to have someone read these relaxation and awareness techniques aloud to you while you follow along with your eyes closed, permitting yourself to enter as deep a state of relaxation as you can.

For superior results, I suggest that you prerecord the following exercises in your *own* voice, then play the tape back so that you can serve as your own guide. And don't give any credence to that old fear about going into a trance and sleeping on and on like Rip Van Winkle. If you should fall into an altered state of consciousness while listening to your previously recorded exercises, you will simply awaken within a brief time, just as you would from any normal sleep.

You will also find that these techniques will be most effective for you if you select a time of day when you know that you will not be disturbed. Find a quiet place where you will not be bothered by anyone, so that you may lie down or sit comfortably or assume a yogic or meditative posture.

An Easy Technique to Bring About a State of Relaxation:

In addition to recording this relaxation technique so that you can play it back to allow your own voice to guide you, you might also wish to play some soft restful music—free of lyrics—in the background. Read the following relaxation technique in a soft, slow, measured—but confident—voice:

Imagine that you are lying or sitting in a place that you consider especially beautiful, peaceful, relaxing. A blanket near the beach . . . a soft bed of leaves near a gently moving brook . . . a bench overlooking a lovely mountain view. Wherever you wish . . . you are there. Wherever you wish . . . you are relaxing, relaxing, relaxing.

As you relax, you know that nothing will disturb you, nothing will distress you, nothing will molest or bother you in any way. Even now you are becoming aware of a peaceful feeling of love that is moving over you, protecting you.

You know that you have nothing to fear. Nothing can harm you.

As you listen to the sound of my voice, you feel all tension leaving your body. The sound of my voice helps you to become more and more relaxed.

With every breath you take, you find yourself feeling better and more at peace. You must permit your body to relax so that you can rise to higher states of consciousness.

Your body must relax so that the Real You may rise higher and higher to greater states of awareness.

You are feeling a beautiful energy of tranquility, peace, and love entering your feet; and you feel every muscle in your feet relaxing.

That beautiful energy of tranquility, peace, and love moves up your legs . . . into your ankles . . . your calves . . . your knees . . . your thighs; and you feel every muscle in your ankles . . . your calves . . . your knees . . . your thighs, relaxing, relaxing, relaxing.

If you should hear any sound at all—a slamming door . . . a honking horn . . . a shouting voice—that sound will not disturb you. That sound will only help to relax you even more.

Nothing will disturb you. Nothing will distress you in any way.

And now that beautiful energy of tranquility, peace, and love is moving up to your hips . . . your stomach . . . your back; and you feel every muscle in your hips . . . your stomach . . . your back . . . relaxing, relaxing, relaxing.

With every breath you take, you find that your body is becoming more and more relaxed.

And now that beautiful energy of tranquility, peace, and love enters your chest . . . your shoulders . . . your arms . . . even your fingers. And you feel every muscle in your chest . . . your shoulders . . . your arms . . . and your fingers relaxing, relaxing, relaxing.

And with every breath that you take you find that you are becoming more . . . and more . . . relaxed. Every part of your body is becoming relaxed, free of tension.

Now that beautiful energy of tranquility, peace, and love moves into your neck . . . your face . . . the very top of your head. And you feel every muscle in your neck . . . your face . . . and the very top of your head relaxing . . . relaxing . . . relaxing . . . relaxing.

Your body is now relaxed, but your mind, your spirit, your soul—your True Self—is very aware.

Once the body is relaxed, proceed with the following exercise:

Meeting Your Spiritual Guide

And now a beautiful golden globe of light is moving toward you.

You are not afraid, for you realize, you *know,* that within the golden globe of light is your spiritual guide, your guardian angel, who has loved you since *before* you became you.

Feel the love as this beautiful presence comes

closer to you. Feel the vibrations of love moving over you—warm, peaceful, tranquil.

You know that within this golden globe of light is someone who has always loved you just as you are.

You have been aware of this loving, guiding presence ever since you were a small child.

You have been aware that this intelligence has always loved you with Heavenly Love.

You have always known that your angel guide has loved you unconditionally with Heavenly Love.

You feel that love moving all around you.

And look! Two eyes are beginning to form in the midst of the golden light. Those are the eyes of your angel guide. Feel the love flowing to you from your angel guide.

Now a face is forming. Oh, look at the smile on the lips of your angel guide. Feel the love that flows from your angel guide to you.

Now a body is forming. Behold the beauty of form, structure, and stature of your angel guide.

Feel the love that flows to you from the very presence of your angel guide.

Your angel guide is now stretching forth a loving hand to you. Take that hand in yours. Life up your hand and accept your angel guide's hand into yours.

Feel the love flowing through you. *Feel* the love as you and your angel guide blend and flow together.

Feel the wonderful warmth and glow of Divine Love as you and your angel become One with the Heavenly Light!

You may now move directly into the next exercise:

Viewing the Heavenly Kingdom

Now, hand in hand, you feel yourself being lifted higher and higher. Your angel guide is now taking you to that other dimension for which you have always longed.

You are moving higher, higher, higher.

Colors and lights are moving past you . . . red . . . orange . . . yellow . . . green . . . blue . . . violet . . . gold . . . purple.

You are moving into another dimension of time and space.

You are moving into a higher vibration.

You are moving toward a place of higher awareness, of higher consciousness.

At the count of three, you will arrive in that higher dimension. One . . . two . . . *three!*

You have now arrived at that place for which you have always yearned.

Look around you. The trees, grass, sky— *everything* is more alive. The colors are more vivid here.

And look at you! You, too, have been transformed. It is as if you suddenly have a new nervous system.

You have new eyes to see those things that you have never seen before.

You have new ears to hear sounds and voices that you have never heard before.

You are clothed in a robe of white with a golden cord tied around your middle. Sandals are on your feet.

And look ahead. *See the beautiful crystal kingdom!*

A marvelous golden light is reflecting from every tower, every spire, every turret, every wall.

You *know* where you are! You've come to visit your true home in this beautiful, spiritual dimension.

Look at the people coming to greet you.

Look at their eyes.

Feel their love.

You recognize so many of them.

Some are dear ones from the Earth plane who have already returned to their true home beyond the stars.

They reach out to touch you, to embrace you, to kiss you. And you feel their love flowing all around you.

As you follow your angel guide through the crystal city, you feel love all around you. Love as you have never felt it on Earth. Love as you have yearned for all of your life.

And you feel it now, all around you.

As you walk through the beautiful streets, you see that your angel guide is leading you to a marvelous golden temple of Love, Wisdom, and Knowledge.

There is a beautiful garden ahead. See the trees heavy with fruit. See the incredible array of colorful flowers. Smell the air, sweet as spring honey.

There is a lovely silver stream that runs at the foot of the nine golden steps that lead to the great door of the Temple of Love, Wisdom, and Knowledge.

Take your angel guide's hand and begin to walk up the nine golden steps. One by one, feel the steps beneath your sandals. One . . . two . . . three . . . four . . . five . . . six . . . seven . . . eight . . . *nine*.

The great golden door opens, and you step inside.

Look at the magnificent tapestry that covers the wall to your left. This tapestry reminds you that you are a single, but very important, thread that runs throughout the great fabric of life in the universe.

And now behold the altar! There are thousands of little candles burning and glowing before the beautiful golden altar.

Beyond the altar, you perceive a Light that glows with such brilliant intensity that you cannot stare at it with even your spiritual eyes.

You know that this is the Holy of Holies . . . the Divine Light, the creative energy that sustains the very center of the universe.

A shaft of golden light shoots toward you from the Divine Light, and you feel a powerful surge of love and well-being permeate your entire spiritual being. You feel an energy of peace and love that you know will energize your spirit and sustain your physical body.

And now your angel guide is telling you that it is time to return to Earth. It is time to return to full wakefulness in your physical body.

But you know that you may return to the Temple of Love, Wisdom, and Knowledge in the crystal city in the Heavenly Kingdom as often as you deem it necessary for your good and your gaining.

You know that you may return to receive the beautiful reinforcement of this love vibration as often as you require it.

And you know that your angel guide is always with you.

At the count of five you will return to full wakefulness in your physical body.

You will feel better in mind, body, and spirit than you have felt in weeks and weeks, months and months.

One . . . beginning to come awake.

Two . . . coming more and more awake.

Three . . . opening your eyes.

Four . . . stretching and moving.

Five . . . wide awake and feeling wonderful! Wide awake and feeling filled with love, wisdom, and knowledge.

Why Are So Many People Having Near-Death and Other Mystical Experiences?

The reason why so many men and women are beginning to take notice of such phenomena as the near-death experience, angels, and other mystical occurrences may be due to the fact that in the Western world our nonrational needs have been denied for decades. Materialism, competition, power politics, and commercial exploitation can be endured for only so long before the human soul cries out for meaningful spiritual expression.

The increase in such experiences may also be due to a time of great transition which many sensitive men and women feel is fast approaching. Some perceive that our entire human species may be standing on the precipice of a great leap forward in our physical and spiritual evolution.

Although the Western world has never encouraged the individual mystical experience, for those of us who collect such accounts as you have read in this book, it seems clear that we are all potential mystics, just as there are potential artists, poets, and musicians.

The philosopher-psychologist William James once observed that the Mother Sea, the fountainhead of all religions, lies in the mystical experience of the individual. All theologies, all ecclesiastical establishments are but secondary growths superimposed upon the initial revelatory experience.

If you should become one of those individuals who undergoes a near-death or illumination experience, a touch of cosmic consciousness, or a revelation from Divine Light, it shall hence forth truly be said of you that by your works, you shall be known.

You will develop deeper qualities of understanding.

You will demonstrate diminished concern about the selfish interests of the world.

You will gain a deep sense of peace and freedom.

You will achieve a powerful sense of wholeness and of Oneness with the cosmos.

You will notice a great shift in consciousness from self to other, from "I" to "thou," from "mine" to "ours."

You will find that your physical health will manifest in increased vitality.

You will develop a much greater patience toward your mission in life.

You will be consumed with desire to fulfill universal laws directed at cosmic harmony.

You will understand that your soul is both individual and universal.

You will become totally aware that there is a higher intelligence from which you may draw power, strength, and inspiration.

And, of course, you will no longer fear death.

As the great Yogi and mystic Parmahansa Yogananda phrased it (*Where There Is Light*): "Death is only an experience through which you are meant to learn a great lesson: you cannot die."